CW01494991

A Practical Guide to

Data Protection Law

in the United Kingdom

ISBN: 9798882962851

MANCUNIA
PUBLISHING

Copyright © 2024 by Mancunia Publishing

All rights reserved. No part of this publication may be reproduced, distributed, or transmitted in any form or by any means, including photocopying, recording, or other electronic or mechanical methods, without the prior written permission of the publisher, except in the case of brief quotations embodied in critical reviews and certain other noncommercial uses permitted by copyright law.

Overview of the Data Protection Act 2018.............................5
Principles of data protection in the UK.................................8
Personal data definition and scope....................................11
Sensitive personal data under the Data Protection Act..... 14
Data subjects' rights under the Data Protection Act.......... 16
Data controllers and data processors................................ 19
Data protection impact assessments................................ 22
Data protection by design and by default...........................25
Data protection officers..28
International data transfers...31
Data breaches and notification requirements....................34
Consent requirements for data processing........................ 37
Legal bases for processing personal data..........................40
Rights and obligations of data subjects.............................43
Data retention and deletion...46
Accountability and governance..49
Data protection in the workplace.......................................52
Children's data protection...55
CCTV and data protection in the UK...................................58
Direct marketing and data protection in the UK.................61
Data protection in healthcare..64
Data protection in education..67
Data protection in financial services................................. 70
Data protection in social media...73
Data protection in research...76
Data protection in law enforcement.................................. 79
Data protection impact on AI and machine learning..........82
Data protection and cloud computing................................85
Data protection and biometrics.. 88
Data protection and cybersecurity.....................................91
Data protection and the GDPR...94

Data protection and human rights..................................97
Data protection and freedom of expression......................100
Data protection and the right to access information....... 103
Data protection and e-commerce.....................................106
Data protection and the Internet of Things (IoT)..............109
Data protection and big data analytics............................ 112
Data protection and government surveillance..................115
Data protection and employment in the UK......................118
Data protection and social responsibility.........................121

Overview of the Data Protection Act 2018

The Data Protection Act 2018 (DPA 2018) is a pivotal piece of legislation in the UK that sets the framework for data protection law. It's an embodiment of the General Data Protection Regulation (GDPR), and it replaced the Data Protection Act of 1998, bringing with it a significant shift in the way that organisations and individuals must handle and process personal data.

The Act applies to 'controllers' and 'processors' of personal data. A controller is an individual or organisation that determines the how and why personal data is processed, while a processor is responsible for processing personal data on behalf of the controller. Both of these entities have specific legal obligations under the Act.

The DPA 2018 categorises personal data into two types: 'personal data' and 'special category data'. Personal data is any information relating to an identifiable living individual, such as name, address, or online identifier. Special category data, on the other hand, refers to more sensitive information that requires higher levels of protection, including data about race, ethnic origin, politics, religion, trade union membership, genetics, biometrics, health, sex life, or sexual orientation.

The Act sets out seven key principles relating to the processing of personal data: lawfulness, fairness, and transparency; purpose limitation; data minimisation; accuracy; storage limitation; integrity and confidentiality (security); and accountability. These principles lie at the heart of the DPA 2018 and are not just theoretical concepts but practical rules that must be put into action.

The principle of lawfulness, fairness, and transparency requires that personal data must be processed lawfully, fairly, and in a transparent manner in relation to individuals. The principle of purpose limitation suggests that personal data should be collected for specified, explicit and legitimate purposes only, and not further processed in a way that is incompatible with those purposes.

The principle of data minimisation asserts that personal data must be adequate, relevant and limited to what is necessary in relation to the purposes for which they are processed. The principle of accuracy requires personal data to be accurate and, where necessary, kept up to date. The storage limitation principle insists that personal data should be kept in a form which permits identification of data subjects for no longer than is necessary for the purposes for which the personal data are processed.

The integrity and confidentiality principle, also known as the security principle, prescribes that personal data must be processed in a manner that ensures appropriate security of the personal data, including protection against unauthorised or unlawful processing and against accidental loss, destruction or damage. Lastly, the accountability principle entails that the data controller is responsible for, and be able to demonstrate compliance with, the other principles.

The DPA 2018 also affirms the rights of individuals concerning their personal data. These rights include the right to be informed, the right of access, the right to rectification, the right to erasure (also known as the 'right to be forgotten'), the right to restrict processing, the right to data portability, the right to object, and rights concerning automated decision making and profiling.

Non-compliance with the DPA 2018 can lead to serious consequences, including hefty fines. The Information

Commissioner's Office (ICO), the supervisory authority in the UK, has the power to take enforcement action against controllers and processors who fail to comply with the Act.

Moreover, DPA 2018 has provisions on the transfer of personal data to other countries or international organisations, ensuring that the level of protection of individuals afforded by the DPA 2018 and the GDPR is not undermined.

Therefore, the Data Protection Act 2018 is an extensive piece of legislation that forms a significant part of the legal framework in the UK for data protection, setting out the rights of individuals and the obligations of data controllers and processors. It also provides for enforcement measures and penalties for non-compliance, ensuring that the fundamental right to privacy, in relation to personal data, is protected.

Principles of data protection in the UK

The guiding principles of data protection in the UK are enshrined in the General Data Protection Regulation (GDPR), which came into force in May 2018 and then incorporated into UK law as UK GDPR after Brexit. These principles are fundamentally aimed at ensuring that individuals' rights are respected in relation to their personal data, and that organisations process such data in a fair, transparent, and lawful manner.

The first principle under UK GDPR stipulates that personal data must be processed lawfully, fairly, and transparently. This principle is at the heart of data protection. Lawful processing refers to the requirement that there needs to be a legal basis for the processing of personal data, such as the necessity of processing for the performance of a contract, compliance with a legal obligation, or the legitimate interests of the data controller. Fair processing means that the data should not be processed in a way that is unduly detrimental, unexpected or misleading to the individuals concerned. The transparency element of this principle requires that clear information is provided about the data processing activities, which is usually achieved through a privacy notice.

The second principle mandates that personal data must be collected for specified, explicit, and legitimate purposes. This indicates that organisations must be clear from the outset about why they are collecting personal data and what they intend to do with it. Importantly, it precludes the possibility of collecting data now and deciding what to do with it later. The purpose must be specific and clear to prevent data use that individuals would not expect or might object to.

The third principle prescribes that personal data should be adequate, relevant, and limited to what is necessary. This principle, also known as data minimisation, means that organisations should only process the data they need for their specified purpose. Excessive data collection is not justifiable and can lead to significant penalties.

The fourth principle demands that personal data must be accurate and, where necessary, kept up to date. Inaccurate data can lead to incorrect decisions being made, and may also cause significant distress to individuals. Therefore, organisations should regularly check the accuracy of the data they hold and take all reasonable steps to correct or erase inaccurate data.

The fifth principle propounds that personal data should be kept in a form which permits identification of data subjects for no longer than is necessary. This principle, known as storage limitation, essentially means that organisations should not keep personal data for longer than they need it. Once the stated purpose is achieved, or the data is no longer required, it should be securely deleted.

The sixth and final principle of the UK GDPR mandates that personal data must be processed in a manner that ensures appropriate security. This includes protection against unauthorised or unlawful processing, accidental loss, destruction or damage. It is incumbent upon organisations to implement robust security measures commensurate with the risks involved, and to regularly test and evaluate the effectiveness of these measures.

The principles are supplemented by the accountability requirement. This new addition to UK GDPR mandates that organisations must be able to demonstrate their compliance with the principles. This could include implementing and maintaining appropriate data protection policies and procedures, undertaking data protection impact assessments where necessary, and appointing a data protection officer in certain circumstances.

It is essential for organisations operating within the UK to adhere strictly to these principles to avoid heavy fines and damage to their reputation. However, beyond these practical considerations, these principles also represent a commitment to respect the fundamental rights and freedoms of individuals in relation to their personal data. These principles, therefore, not only shape how organisations handle data but also contribute to a culture of data protection and privacy within the UK.

Personal data definition and scope

Personal data, as defined by the UK's data protection law, primarily refers to any information that relates to an identifiable living individual. It is an umbrella term used to encapsively describe any sort of data that could potentially be used to identify a person either directly or indirectly. This includes single elements of data or a combination of data sets that can lead to the identification of a person.

This definition is enshrined in the UK's Data Protection Act 2018, which adopts the definition given in the EU General Data Protection Regulation (GDPR). According to this legislation, personal data encompasses a broad spectrum of information. It could range from something as basic as a name or a number, to more intricate forms of data such as the physical, physiological, genetic, mental, economic, cultural or social identity of an individual.

It is important to take note of the phrase 'identifiable living individual'. Here, 'identifiable' signifies that an individual can be directly or indirectly identified by this data. This can be through reference to an identifier like a name, identification number, location data or an online identifier, or to one or more factors specific to the physical, physiological, genetic, mental, economic, cultural or social identity of that individual. Consequently, even if the data does not directly reveal the identity of a person, if it can be combined with other data to identify the individual, it falls under the scope of personal data.

Furthermore, 'living individual' makes it clear that personal data only relates to living persons. Information about deceased individuals does not come under the umbrella of personal data, although some legal protections might be applicable for such data under confidentiality laws.

The scope of personal data also includes 'special category data', which was earlier known as 'sensitive personal data'. This is personal data that is deemed more sensitive and could create significant risks to a person's fundamental rights and freedoms. The special category data comprises information about an individual's race, ethnic origin, political opinions, religious or philosophical beliefs, trade union membership, genetic data, biometric data for uniquely identifying an individual, data concerning health, data about a person's sex life or sexual orientation.

Another important aspect of the definition of personal data in UK legislation is the concept of 'pseudonymised data'. This refers to data that has undergone a process that renders the data subject unidentifiable without the use of additional information. Since this additional information can be used to identify the individual, pseudonymised data is still considered personal data under UK law.

Lastly, in the UK, personal data does not include data related to a legal person such as a limited company, public authority or other bodies corporate. However, data relating to sole traders, partners, and some other types of business entities could be considered personal data if it allows the identification of living individuals.

In conclusion, personal data in the UK constitutes a vast array of information, with the potential to identify an individual being its central characteristic. This data is protected by a robust legal framework, which places stringent obligations on organisations processing personal data, with significant penalties for breaches.

Therefore, understanding the definition and scope of personal data is essential for anyone managing or using such data.

Sensitive personal data under the Data Protection Act

Sensitive personal data under the Data Protection Act 2018 (DPA) in the UK is a category of personal data that requires elevated levels of protection. It pertains to information which, if misused or mishandled, could lead to significant harm or discrimination towards the data subject. The Act provides stringent regulations to ensure that sensitive personal data is treated with the utmost care, and any breaches are taken very seriously.

The Data Protection Act 2018 is the UK's implementation of the General Data Protection Regulation (GDPR) and it categorises sensitive personal data under 'special categories'. This includes data concerning racial and ethnic origin, political opinions, religious beliefs, trade union membership, physical and mental health conditions, sexual orientation, genetic and biometric data, and criminal convictions or offences. It is important to note that these special categories extend the rights of data subjects and place further obligations on data controllers and processors.

Under the Act, the information concerning a data subject must be processed lawfully, fairly, and transparently. For sensitive personal data, this means that in most cases, the data subject must give explicit consent before their data can be processed. The Act provides for certain exceptions where the processing of sensitive personal data is necessary, for instance, for reasons of substantial public interest, legal claims, medical diagnosis, or for the protection of vital interests of the data subject. However, even in these cases, the data controller or processor must take great care to ensure the data is handled appropriately.

The processing of sensitive personal data must also fulfil the principles outlined in the Act. These include limiting the processing to what is necessary for specific, explicit, and legitimate purposes, ensuring the data is accurate and up to date, and retaining the data no longer than necessary. Furthermore, there is a requirement to implement appropriate technical and organisational measures to safeguard sensitive personal data. This could include pseudonymisation or encryption of the data, ensuring the ongoing confidentiality, integrity, availability, and resilience of processing systems and services, and having a procedure in place to respond to any data breaches.

The Act also provides rights for individuals concerning their sensitive personal data. These include the right to be informed about the collection and use of their data, the right to access their data, the right to rectification if their data is inaccurate or incomplete, the right to erasure or 'the right to be forgotten', the right to restrict processing, the right to data portability, the right to object to processing, and rights in relation to automated decision making and profiling.

Data controllers and processors who handle sensitive personal data have a duty to inform the Information Commissioner's Office (ICO) about their processing activities. The ICO is the UK's independent authority set up to uphold information rights in the public interest and to promote openness by public bodies. The ICO has the power to enforce penalties for breaches of the DPA, including hefty fines and sanctions.

In conclusion, the handling of sensitive personal data under the Data Protection Act 2018 in the UK is heavily regulated, with specific guidelines and principles to be adhered to. The Act aims to protect individuals' data privacy rights, and any deviation from these guidelines may lead to serious repercussions.

Data subjects' rights under the Data Protection Act

The Data Protection Act 2018 (DPA 2018) is a comprehensive legislative framework that governs how organisations in the United Kingdom handle personal data. One of the fundamental aspects of the DPA 2018 is empowering data subjects, individuals to whom the data pertains, with specific rights that ensure their data is treated with respect and privacy. These rights serve as the cornerstone of the data protection framework and are designed to enable individuals to maintain control over their personal information.

The first and perhaps the most basic right is the right to be informed. This right requires organisations to provide clear and transparent information about how they use individuals' personal data. The information typically comprises who the data controller is, the purpose for processing the data, the legal basis for processing, who the data will be shared with, and the period for which the data will be stored. Depending on the circumstances, the data subject must be informed whether the provision of personal data is a statutory or contractual requirement, and the possible consequences if the individual fails to provide the personal data.

The second right, the right of access, allows individuals to ascertain whether an organisation is processing their personal data and if so, to request a copy of such data. This right is intended to ensure individuals can verify the lawfulness of the processing and check the accuracy of their data. Furthermore, it allows individuals to establish what personal information an organisation holds about them and why.

The third right, the right to rectification, enables individuals to have inaccurate personal data rectified or completed if it is incomplete. Individuals may exercise this right when the data held about them is incorrect or misleading. In response, the organisation must take every reasonable step to correct or complete the relevant data without delay.

Next comes the right to erasure, often referred to as the right to be forgotten. This right allows individuals to request the deletion or removal of personal data where there is no compelling reason for its continued processing. It applies in specific circumstances, such as where the data is no longer necessary for the purpose it was originally collected, consent has been withdrawn, or the data has been unlawfully processed.

Fifth is the right to restrict processing, which permits individuals to block or suppress the processing of their personal data. In such cases, an organisation may store the personal data, but not further process it. This right is applicable when the individual contests the accuracy of the personal data, the processing is unlawful, the individual objects to the processing, or the organisation no longer needs the personal data for the original purpose but requires it to establish, exercise or defend legal claims.

The sixth right, the right to data portability, allows individuals to obtain and reuse their personal data for their own purposes across different services. This right only applies to personal data that an individual has provided to a controller, where the processing is based on the individual's consent or for the performance of a contract and when processing is carried out by automated means.

The right to object is the seventh right, where individuals have the right to object to processing based on legitimate interests or the performance of a task in the public interest, direct marketing, or processing for purposes of scientific or historical research and statistics.

Finally, the right related to automated decision making and profiling protects individuals in cases where decisions are made by automated means without human involvement. These decisions can be based purely on automated processing, which may include profiling. If an organisation is carrying out wholly automated decision-making process that has legal or similarly significant effects on individuals, it must ensure that certain safeguards are in place.

It is crucial to note that these rights are not absolute and are subject to certain conditions and exemptions. Nonetheless, they offer a robust mechanism for individuals to control the use of their personal data. Organisations are required to inform individuals of these rights at the time of data collection and actively support them in exercising these rights. Failure to comply with these rights may lead to enforcement action by the Information Commissioner's Office (ICO), including hefty fines and penalties. The DPA 2018 thus ensures that data protection is not just an afterthought, but an integral part of the data processing lifecycle.

Data controllers and data processors

In the United Kingdom, the roles of data controllers and data processors are clearly defined in the Data Protection Act 2018, as well as the General Data Protection Regulation (GDPR). These two crucial entities work in tandem to ensure that data privacy rights of individuals are duly respected, and personal data is handled in a secure and lawful manner.

A data controller, as the name implies, exercises control over the 'why' and 'how' personal data is to be processed. This role encompasses the responsibility to determine the purposes and means of processing personal data. In essence, a data controller embarks on the decision-making process regarding the need for data, the categories of data that need to be processed, and the length of time for which the data would be retained. In addition, the data controller is tasked with ensuring that the data processing operations are in line with the data protection principles set out in the GDPR.

Typically, the data controller could be any organisation, from a multinational corporation to a local charity that collects and uses personal data. For instance, a bank, an insurance company, a government department, a university, or an online retailer could all function as data controllers. Therefore, data controllers in the UK are not confined to certain industries or sectors, but manifest across a broad spectrum of organisations, irrespective of their size or nature.

The duties of a data controller are heavy and demand a high level of accountability. They are obliged to implement appropriate technical and organisational measures to ensure data processing is performed in accordance with the GDPR. This could encompass measures such as pseudonymisation and data encryption, maintaining a record of processing activities, conducting impact assessments, and implementing policies that meet the principles of data protection by design and data protection by default. Furthermore, they are accountable for notifying the Information Commissioner's Office (ICO) within 72 hours of recognising a data breach.

Shifting the spotlight to the role of a data processor, this entity processes personal data on behalf of the data controller. The data processor takes its instructions from the controller and carries out the actual data processing work. This could include activities such as data collection, recording, organisation, structuring, storage, adaptation, retrieval, consultation, use, disclosure, erasure, or destruction.

The data processor role is often embodied by third parties that provide specific services to the data controller. These could be IT service providers, payroll companies, market research firms, cloud storage providers, or even accountants, to name a few examples. It is important to note that while the data controller has the overarching responsibility for the data, the processor also has a legal obligation to maintain the integrity of the data they handle and protect it from theft, loss, or accidental destruction.

Both the data controller and the data processor are bound by contractual agreements, which should clearly stipulate the scope, duration, nature, and purpose of the data processing, the types of personal data involved, and the obligations and rights of the data controller.

The ICO, the UK's independent authority set up to uphold information rights, sets stringent measures for both data controllers and processors. Non-compliance can lead to hefty fines. Therefore, understanding the duties and responsibilities of each role and ensuring strict adherence to them is not just a legal obligation, but also a practical necessity in maintaining the trust and confidence of individuals whose data is being processed. This ultimately contributes to the smooth functioning of the data-driven world that we live in today.

Data protection impact assessments

Data protection impact assessments (DPIAs), as mandated by the General Data Protection Regulation (GDPR) and the UK Data Protection Act of 2018, play an integral role in the UK's regulatory landscape, offering proactive and preventative measures to protect personal data. The primary purpose of these assessments is to identify and minimise the data protection risks inherent to specific projects, fostering an environment that promotes accountability and transparency.

DPIAs act as a form of risk assessment, specifically designed for data protection. They are required when data processing activities could result in high risks to the rights and freedoms of individuals. Such activities might include systematic and extensive profiling with significant effects or large-scale processing of special category data. It is important to note that not all projects necessitate a DPIA. However, carrying out an assessment even when it is not explicitly required is often considered good practice.

The process of conducting a DPIA in the UK involves several interconnected stages that collectively offer a comprehensive assessment of the potential risks and mitigation steps. Initially, the need for a DPIA is determined, which will involve understanding the nature, scope, context and purpose of the processing. Following this, information is gathered about the processing operations, where thorough documentation can aid in mapping out the data flows.

Subsequently, the potential risks to individuals are assessed in terms of both their likelihood and severity. It is crucial to remember that risks may not only be related to privacy but could also encompass other potential harms, such as social or economic disadvantage. A crucial part of conducting a DPIA is consulting with those who could be impacted by the processing. This consultation process can range from informal discussions to formal surveys or public consultations.

Once the risks have been identified, the next stage involves determining the measures that can be taken to mitigate these risks. When considering potential safeguards, it can be beneficial to draw upon relevant standards or guidance. Once these measures have been implemented, the DPIA should reassess the level of risk. If the risk is still too high, consultation with the UK's data protection authority, the Information Commissioner's Office (ICO), must be sought.

The ICO's role within the DPIA process is crucial. If an organisation cannot sufficiently diminish the identified risks and decides to proceed nonetheless, it must consult the ICO before processing. After receiving such consultation, the ICO has the power to provide written advice or even to use its enforcement powers if it considers the intended processing would infringe the GDPR.

The final, ongoing stage of the DPIA process is integration and review. The DPIA should be integrated into the project plan and continually reviewed and updated as necessary. This iterative approach ensures that the DPIA remains relevant and effective as the project evolves.

In sum, DPIAs, under the auspices of the UK's data protection legal framework, represent a holistic and strategic approach to ensuring data processing projects are conducted in a manner that respects the rights and freedoms of individuals. They serve as a critical tool for organisations to display accountability and transparency, fostering trust with the public and regulatory bodies alike.

Data protection by design and by default

In the United Kingdom, data protection by design and by default is an integral part of the General Data Protection Regulation (GDPR), adapted by the UK through the Data Protection Act of 2018. This principle is deeply rooted in the concept of embedding data protection from the onset of the designing of systems, rather than as an addition.

Data protection by design is essentially a proactive approach to data privacy. It entails the integration of data privacy principles right from the earliest stages of project conceptualisation or system development. In the UK, this approach is primarily encapsulated within the GDPR's Article 25. It encourages businesses, institutions and organisations to consider privacy during the initial design phases of projects and throughout the complete lifecycle of the relevant data processing. The Information Commissioner's Office (ICO), the UK's regulatory body for data protection, advocates for the implementation of such principles, offering guidelines on how to incorporate this approach into various practices.

Data protection by design necessitates that privacy settings must be set at a high level by default. This is essentially what the 'by default' part of the principle emphasises. It requires that only necessary data should be processed, stored or collected, and that such data should not be accessible without the individual's explicit consent. The principle applies to the amount of personal data collected, the extent of their processing, the period of their storage and their accessibility. In simpler terms, personal data should not be made publicly available without the individual's informed consent.

In the UK, adhering to the principles of data protection by default and by design is not just a mere recommendation, but a legal requirement. The Data Protection Act 2018 compels organisations and businesses to implement appropriate technical and organisational measures to ensure that, by default, only personal data necessary for each specific purpose of the processing is processed. This includes the obligation to hold and process only the data absolutely necessary for the completion of its duties, as well as the obligation to limit the access to personal data to those needing to act out the processing.

The UK's data protection regulation also provides detailed guidelines on conducting Privacy Impact Assessments (PIAs). These are tools which can help organisations identify the most effective way to comply with their data protection obligations and meet individuals' expectations of privacy. An effective PIA will allow organisations to identify and fix problems at an early stage, reducing the associated costs and damage to reputation which might otherwise occur.

To further safeguard data subjects, the UK insists on the use of pseudonymisation, a data management procedure where personally identifiable information fields in a data record are replaced by artificial identifiers, or pseudonyms. This effectively reduces the risk of data breaches as even in case of a breach, the data obtained would be of little or no use without the key to associate it with an individual.

The 'by design and by default' principle reflected in the UK's approach to data protection, therefore, is one that prioritises proactive measures, risk identification and mitigation, legal compliance, and the upholding of individuals' privacy rights. It is a comprehensive strategy aimed at ensuring responsible, transparent and minimalistic handling of personal data. It is also a reflection of the UK's commitment to preserving the trust and confidence of individuals in how their personal data is used and protected.

Data protection officers

Data protection officers, often abbreviated as DPOs, hold a crucial role within organisations in the United Kingdom. In the data-driven world we inhabit, the importance and relevance of such professionals cannot be overstated. In essence, DPOs are tasked with the responsibility of ensuring that their organisations follow the stringent data protection laws laid down by the UK government and the European Union, such as the General Data Protection Regulation (GDPR).

Their remit extends to a wide array of duties and responsibilities, particularly in businesses and organisations where the processing of personal data is a core activity. As such, these professionals are expected to be well-versed in the legal framework that governs data protection in both the domestic and international spheres.

In particular, DPOs are tasked with monitoring an organisation's data protection strategy and its implementation to ensure compliance with GDPR rules. They are required to train staff involved in data processing and conduct regular security audits to safeguard against potential breaches. One of their key roles also involves serving as the point of contact between the company and any Supervisory Authorities (SAs) that oversee data protection law's adherence.

A DPO needs to have a thorough understanding of both technical and organisational measures to maintain data protection. They need to ensure data protection by design and by default, meaning data protection measures should be integrated into the processing activities and business practices right from the design stage.

DPOs in the UK might also be responsible for maintaining comprehensive records of all data processing activities conducted by the company, including the purpose of all processing activities, which must be made public on request. They must also cooperate with the Information Commissioner's Office (ICO), the UK's independent authority set up to uphold information rights in the public interest, promoting openness by public bodies and data privacy for individuals.

While their primary role is to enable the organisation to process personal data lawfully, they also act as mediators between data subjects, the organisation and the authorities. In cases when individuals wish to exercise their rights under the GDPR, the DPO steps in to ensure these rights are duly respected.

It is also worth noting that DPOs ought to be appointed on the basis of their professional qualities and, in particular, expert knowledge on data protection law and practices. This underscores the high level of expertise required to navigate the intricate labyrinth of data protection regulations in the UK and the EU at large.

A unique aspect of the position of DPOs within an organisation is their independent status. They should not receive any instructions regarding the exercise of their tasks and must not be dismissed or penalised for performing their duties. They directly report to the highest level of management and are given the necessary resources to carry out their responsibilities effectively.

In summary, the role of Data Protection Officers in the UK is both critical and complex. They are the pillars on which the edifice of data protection in an organisation rests, ensuring the lawful and ethical use of personal data. Their role is multifaceted – encompassing everything from the execution of strategy and training of staff to dealing with breaches and liaising with authorities. These professionals, armed with extensive knowledge of data protection laws, technical understanding and the ability to engage with key stakeholders, are key in steering their organisations safely through the intricate waters of data protection regulation. As such, their significance within any data-driven organisation in the United Kingdom cannot be overstated.

International data transfers

International data transfers are a central issue under the Data Protection Act 2018, the principal law governing data protection in the United Kingdom. This Act incorporates and supplements the EU's General Data Protection Regulation (GDPR) to reflect the UK's PECR (Privacy and Electronic Communications Regulations) and applies to all companies that process personal data about individuals in the UK.

Fundamentally, international data transfers under the Data Protection Act 2018 involve the movement of personal data from the UK to a third country or international organisation. This transfer of data must uphold the high standards of data protection present in the UK, even when it leaves the country's borders. The Act outlines stringent measures to protect the rights of data subjects during these transfers, ensuring that personal data is treated with the same level of protection as it would be within the UK.

The Data Protection Act 2018 stipulates that such transfers can only occur if the third country or international organisation guarantees an adequate level of protection. The European Commission is responsible for determining adequacy decisions, assessing whether the data protection measures in place in these regions match up to the standards set by the GDPR. At present, several countries have received an adequacy decision, including Switzerland, Canada, and New Zealand. These countries have demonstrated a robust data protection framework, offering safeguards comparable to those provided under the GDPR.

However, when no adequacy decision exists, organisations must put additional safeguards in place to uphold the rights of UK data subjects. These might include Standard Contractual Clauses (SCCs), approved by the European Commission, which establish data protection obligations for both the data sender and receiver. Alternatively, organisations could adopt Binding Corporate Rules (BCRs), which allow multinational corporations to transfer personal data within the group while ensuring an adequate level of data protection.

Under the Data Protection Act 2018, the Information Commissioner's Office (ICO) plays a critical role in overseeing international data transfers. The ICO provides guidance and support to organisations, helping them understand their obligations under the law. Furthermore, the ICO is empowered to take enforcement action where necessary, ensuring compliance with the Act's provisions.

The Act also recognises the importance of data subjects' rights in relation to international data transfers. It upholds the principles of transparency and accountability, requiring organisations to inform individuals if their data will be transferred overseas and to provide them with an opportunity to object. The Act also upholds individuals' rights to access their personal data, to rectify inaccuracies, and to erase data or restrict its processing in certain circumstances.

However, the Data Protection Act 2018 does make some exceptions for international data transfers in specific situations. For instance, a transfer may be allowed without an adequacy decision or additional safeguards if the transfer is necessary for important reasons of public interest, or for the establishment, exercise or defence of legal claims.

The impact of Brexit on international data transfers under the Data Protection Act 2018 has been a critical concern for many organisations. The UK government seeks to maintain the free flow of data between the UK and the EU and has indicated that transfers of data to the EU will not be restricted. Meanwhile, the EU has initiated its process for assessing the UK's data protection framework for an adequacy decision.

In conclusion, international data transfers under the Data Protection Act 2018 require careful consideration of data protection standards and individuals' rights. Robust measures, diligent oversight by the ICO, and clear obligations for organisations all work together to ensure the secure, lawful, and fair treatment of personal data as it crosses international borders.

Data breaches and notification requirements

Data breaches, an inadvertent or unlawful disclosure, alteration, loss, destruction, or access to personal data transmitted, stored or processed, have become an increasing concern in the United Kingdom. The advent of digitisation has made it easier for cybercriminals to access sensitive personal data, creating a dire need for stringent notification requirements and protective measures.

In the United Kingdom, the Data Protection Act 2018 (DPA 2018) and the General Data Protection Regulation (GDPR), which came into force in May 2018, govern data breaches and notification requirements. Both legal frameworks aim to protect the rights and freedoms of individuals and maintain their privacy by ensuring that their data is handled responsibly.

According to the GDPR, if a data breach occurs, the data controller is obliged to notify the Information Commissioner's Office (ICO), the UK's supervisory authority for data protection issues, without undue delay and, where feasible, not later than 72 hours after having become aware of the breach. This notification obligation applies when the breach is likely to result in a risk to the rights and freedoms of natural persons. In other words, the breach could lead to physical, material, or non-material damage to individuals such as loss of control over their personal data, discrimination, identity theft or fraud, financial loss, unauthorised reversal of pseudonymisation, damage to reputation, or other significant economic or social disadvantage.

The notification to the ICO must include, as a minimum, the nature of the personal data breach, including the categories and approximate number of data subjects and personal data records concerned. It should also include a description of the likely consequences of the personal data breach, measures taken or proposed by the controller to address the breach, and contact details where more information can be obtained.

Further, where a data breach is likely to result in a high risk to the rights and freedoms of individuals, the data controller also has a duty to communicate the breach to the data subject without undue delay. The communication should be in clear and plain language and should contain the same elements as the notification to the ICO. However, there are exceptions to this. Communication to the data subject is not required if the data controller has implemented appropriate technical and organisational protection measures, and those measures were applied to the personal data affected by the breach, in particular, those rendering the data unintelligible to any person not authorised to access it, such as encryption.

Moreover, the data controller can avoid the requirement to communicate a data breach to the data subject if it would involve disproportionate effort. In such a situation, a public communication or similar measure can be used to inform the data subjects effectively. Alternatively, communication to the data subject is not required if the data controller has taken subsequent measures that ensure that the high risk to the rights and freedoms of the data subject is no longer likely to materialise.

In the UK, the ICO has the power to issue monetary penalties of up to £20 million or 4% of an organisation's total worldwide annual turnover of the preceding financial year, whichever is higher, for a breach of these requirements.

It is noteworthy that under the DPA 2018, public authorities and bodies, and specified organisations and businesses, need to appoint a Data Protection Officer (DPO). The DPO is responsible for monitoring compliance with data protection laws, training staff, carrying out internal audits, and being the first point of contact for the ICO and individuals whose data is processed.

In conclusion, data breaches and notification requirements in the UK are regulated by a robust legal framework comprising the GDPR and DPA 2018, aiming to protect individuals' rights and freedoms, prevent unauthorized access to data, and ensure that data controllers handle data responsibly. Failure to comply with these requirements can result in severe penalties, hence the importance for organisations and businesses to have rigorous data protection measures and procedures in place.

Consent requirements for data processing

In the United Kingdom, regulations concerning consent requirements for data processing are governed by the General Data Protection Regulation (GDPR) and the Data Protection Act 2018. These legal frameworks stipulate stringent standards of consent, which are fundamentally tied to the protection of individuals' rights and freedoms in relation to their personal data.

Consent, according to these regulations, is not a vague or open-ended term. It is defined as any freely given, specific, informed, and unambiguous indication of the data subject's wishes by which he or she, by a statement or by a clear affirmative action, signifies agreement to the processing of personal data relating to him or her. This implies that consent must be active, rather than passive, and that silence, pre-ticked boxes or inactivity does not constitute consent.

To ensure compliance with these stringent standards, organisations must be able to demonstrate that the individual has consented to the processing of their data, meaning that they may need to produce evidence of this consent if challenged.

Under GDPR, the requirement for consent to be 'freely given' is particularly significant. This means that individuals must have genuine choice and control over how their data is used. If an individual feels compelled to give consent under any form of duress, or if the performance of a contract is conditional on consent despite the fact that this consent is not strictly necessary for the performance of the contract, such consent will not be considered 'freely given'.

Consent must also be 'specific'. This means that blanket consent, in the absence of specifics about the intended processing, is insufficient. Organisations must ensure that consent is sought separately for different processing activities, which means that consent must not be bundled together for numerous processing activities. Furthermore, where the processing has multiple purposes, consent should be granted for each of those purposes.

The requirement for consent to be 'informed' means that individuals must at the very least be informed of the identity of the organisation processing the data, the purpose for which the data will be used, the type of data to be collected and used, and the individual's right to withdraw consent at any time. The information provided should be concise, transparent, intelligible and easily accessible, and it should be communicated in clear and plain language.

Lastly, for consent to be 'unambiguous', it must involve a clear affirmative action. This can take the form of a written statement, including by electronic means, or an oral statement. This could include ticking a box when visiting an Internet website, choosing technical settings for information society services or another statement or conduct which clearly indicates in this context the data subject's acceptance of the proposed processing of his or her personal data.

In addition to these requirements, the GDPR introduces more stringent requirements for obtaining consent from children for online services. Parental consent will be required for the processing of personal data of children under the age of 13 years. For children aged 13 to 15 years, member states may decide to lower the age limit for consent as long as it is not below 13 years.

Moreover, it is essential to note that individuals have the right to withdraw their consent at any time. It must be as easy to withdraw consent as it was to give it. When consent is withdrawn, all processing activity on the individual's data must cease, unless there is another lawful basis for the processing.

Breaching these regulations can lead to substantial financial penalties, with organisations risking fines of up to 4% of annual global turnover or €20 million, whichever is higher. As such, compliance with the consent requirements for data processing in the UK is not only a matter of ethical data management, but also a fundamental business concern.

Legal bases for processing personal data

In the United Kingdom, the processing of personal data is regulated by the Data Protection Act 2018 (DPA 2018), which incorporates the EU's General Data Protection Regulation (GDPR) into UK law. The DPA 2018 and the GDPR stand as two of the most vital legal frameworks governing the processing of personal data, setting forth various lawful bases for data handling. These legal bases, crucial to any data processing activity, allow organisations, enterprises, and individuals to lawfully process personal data, provided they adhere to specific conditions stipulated within the law.

A key basis for lawful data processing is the provision of consent. This refers to situations where the data subject has freely given, specific, informed, and unambiguous indication of their wishes, either through a statement or a clear affirmative action, that they agree to the processing of their personal data. To fully adhere to this legal basis, organisations must ensure that the consent they acquire is demonstrable, that the individual has a genuine choice, and that they can withdraw their consent at any time.

Another lawful basis for processing personal data is the necessity to perform a contract. Here, organisations can process personal data when it is required to fulfil contractual obligations or to take steps at the request of the data subject before entering into a contract. For instance, a mobile phone company may need to process a customer's home address to deliver the purchased product, thus fulfilling the contract's conditions.

The third legal basis is compliance with a legal obligation. This refers to instances where processing of personal data is necessary for compliance with a legal obligation to which the data controller is subject. For example, an employer may be required by employment law to process employee data for tax purposes.

Processing that is necessary to protect the vital interests of the data subject or of another person also constitutes a lawful basis. This provision is primarily intended for processing personal data in 'life or death' situations, such as when an individual's medical history is required during emergency hospital treatment.

There is also a basis for processing personal data in the public interest or in the exercise of official authority. Public bodies often rely on this basis to process personal data when carrying out tasks that are laid down by law or in the public interest.

Furthermore, there is a legal basis for processing personal data when it is necessary for the purposes of legitimate interests pursued by the data controller or a third party, except where such interests are overridden by the interests or fundamental rights and freedoms of the data subject. This basis is not available to processing carried out by public authorities in the performance of their tasks. The 'legitimate interests' basis is the most flexible among the lawful bases for processing, but it is not a free pass for organisations and demands careful consideration and balancing of the benefits of the processing against the impact on the individual's privacy.

Finally, under conditions defined by law, special category data such as racial or ethnic origin, political opinions, religious or philosophical beliefs, or trade union membership, and the processing of genetic data, biometric data for the purpose of uniquely identifying a natural person, health data, or data concerning a natural person's sex life or sexual orientation may be processed.

Each of these legal bases carries its own stipulations and requirements, and it is incumbent on data controllers to ensure they fully understand and comply with these provisions. Furthermore, in all cases, data controllers are required to meet key principles of data protection, including data minimisation, purpose limitation, accuracy, storage limitation, integrity and confidentiality. Data controllers are also obliged to respect the rights of data subjects, including the right to access their personal data, have it rectified or erased, restrict its processing, and object to its processing.

Rights and obligations of data subjects

In the United Kingdom, the Data Protection Act of 2018, which implements the European General Data Protection Regulation (GDPR) in UK law, serves as a cornerstone in regulating the complex sphere of data protection, particularly focusing on the rights and obligations of data subjects. A data subject is a natural person whose personal data is processed by a controller or processor. The Act ensures a degree of control for people over their personal information and underpins their rights and obligations in relation to the processing of their data.

Data subjects in the UK have a variety of rights under the Data Protection Act. Firstly, they are endowed with the right of access, permitting them to demand a copy of their personal data from organisations. This right enables them to confirm the lawfulness of data processing and verify the accuracy of their personal data, providing a crucial check against misuse or mishandling of information.

Secondly, data subjects possess the right to rectification, allowing them to request modifications to their personal data if they believe it is inaccurate or incomplete. This right is particularly important as it enables individuals to maintain accuracy and relevance of their personal information, ensuring that the data held about them is up-to-date.

Additionally, the right to erasure, often referred to as the 'right to be forgotten', permits individuals to request the deletion or removal of personal data under certain circumstances. This could be when the data is no longer necessary for the purpose it was originally collected for, or when the individual withdraws consent for its processing, provided there is no overriding legitimate reason for retaining it.

The right to restrict processing is also granted to the data subjects. In specific circumstances, they can demand that an organisation stops processing their data. This right applies, for example, when an individual disputes the accuracy of the personal data or objects to processing based on legitimate interests pursued by the organisation.

Data subjects also have the right to data portability. This right allows individuals to obtain and reuse their personal data across different services, facilitating their ability to move, copy or transfer personal data easily from one IT environment to another in a safe and secure manner, without affecting its usability.

Another significant right is the right to object. This allows data subjects to oppose the processing of their personal data in certain circumstances, such as direct marketing or for reasons related to their particular situation. If the data subject objects, the organisation must stop processing their data unless they can demonstrate compelling legitimate grounds for the processing.

The rights related to automated decision making, including profiling, form another crucial aspect of the rights of the data subjects. The Act ensures that individuals have the right not to be subject to a decision based solely on automated processing, including profiling, which has legal or similarly significant effects on them.

In addition to these rights, data subjects also have specific obligations. They are required to provide accurate and up-to-date information to the data controller, and to inform the data controller of any changes to this information. They also have an obligation to exercise their rights responsibly and not misuse them to unjustifiably obstruct data processing operations or inundate organisations with unnecessary requests.

Moreover, data subjects have an obligation to respect the rights of others in the data protection context. This includes respecting the confidentiality of others' information and not infringing upon others' privacy rights when exercising their own data protection rights.

Data subjects also need to cooperate with the data controller and data protection authorities in case of any dispute or issues concerning the processing of their personal data. This includes responding to requests for information or clarifications, and complying with the decisions of data protection authorities regarding their complaints.

The UK Data Protection Act thus provides a comprehensive framework for the rights and obligations of data subjects, aiming to balance the individual's right to privacy with the legitimate interests of organisations in processing personal data. While it empowers individuals to control their personal information, it also imposes certain obligations on them to ensure the effective operation of the data protection regime.

Data retention and deletion

In the United Kingdom, data retention and deletion are governed by various legislative frameworks, chiefly the Data Protection Act 2018 (DPA) and the General Data Protection Regulation (GDPR). These sets of laws provide a robust set of rules for organisations, be they public or private entities, to adhere to when dealing with personal data of individuals.

Data retention refers to the practice of storing data for a predetermined period of time for certain purposes, such as compliance with state regulations or for business requirements. This could involve an array of data types, ranging from financial records and employee details to customer data. As such, it is imperative that a rigorous and concise data retention policy is implemented by each organisation.

The GDPR, in particular, impacts the way data retention is carried out in the UK. It stipulates that personal data should not be kept longer than necessary in relation to the purpose for which such data is processed. However, this 'necessary' timeframe is not fixed and could vary depending on the nature of the data and the purpose for which it is being processed. For example, tax-related data generally need to be kept for six years, but data that is only necessary for short-term marketing campaigns may only need to be kept for a few months.

In addition to the time frame, it is also crucial that the data retention policy outlines the type of data to be retained. Different types of data might have different retention periods depending on their sensitivity and the potential risks associated with their retention. For instance, personal data revealing racial or ethnic origin, political opinions, religious beliefs, or trade union membership, and the processing of genetic data, biometric data for the purpose of uniquely identifying a natural person, data concerning health or data concerning a natural person's sex life or sexual orientation are considered special category data under the GDPR. Such data demands more stringent measures and may have a different retention period than general personal data.

Conversely, data deletion is as crucial as data retention. Secure deletion of data is an essential part of data management, ensuring that the data is irretrievably destroyed when it is no longer needed. Deletion must be undertaken in such a way that the data can no longer be reconstructed by any means. To this end, organisations might use overwriting techniques or physical destruction methods to ensure that the data is effectively rendered unreadable.

Organisations must also consider the 'right to erasure' or 'right to be forgotten' under the GDPR. This provides individuals with the right to have their data deleted in certain circumstances, such as when the data is no longer needed for the purpose for which it was originally collected, or when the individual withdraws their consent for its processing.

In light of the GDPR requirements, organisations are required to carefully document their data retention and deletion policies, and make these policies accessible to individuals whose data they are processing. The policies should clearly define the lifespan of different types of data, the reasons for their retention, the secure methods used for their deletion, and the individuals' rights in relation to their data.

In order to maintain compliance with the data retention and deletion requirements, many organisations have implemented data governance programmes. These programmes typically involve regular audits and reviews of the data held by the organisation, staff training on the importance of data protection and how to handle data securely, and a clear process for responding to data protection requests from individuals.

Notably, non-compliance with the data retention and deletion rules mandated by the DPA and GDPR can result in significant penalties, including hefty fines, for organisations. Therefore, a sound understanding of these rules is essential for any business operating within the UK.

In conclusion, the practices of data retention and deletion in the UK, guided by the DPA and GDPR, are multifaceted, and organisations need to be diligent in their adherence to these principles. The key lies in striking a balance: holding onto data for as long as it is needed, but no longer, and ensuring its secure and effective deletion when that time comes.

Accountability and governance

Accountability and governance fundamentally underpin the principles of data protection in the UK, ensuring that data management abides by the prescribed regulatory standards, respects individual rights and freedoms, procures trust, and is executed with transparency and integrity. The Data Protection Act 2018 (DPA 2018), which incorporates the General Data Protection Regulation (GDPR), forms the crux of the data governance landscape in the UK, obliging organisations to imbue accountability into their data processing activities.

Accountability in data protection envelopes a wide range of measures. It necessitates organisations to not only comply with the principles of data protection but also demonstrate this compliance proactively. This includes mapping the flow of data, carrying out risk assessments, creating data protection policies, implementing data protection by design and default, and appointing a data protection officer (DPO) if mandated. This continual, demonstrable compliance is the heart of accountability in data protection and a vital aspect of good governance.

Notably, the DPA 2018 has significantly expanded the scope of accountability. It demands organisations to maintain detailed records of their data processing activities. These records must include the type of data held, the purpose of processing, to whom it may be disclosed, and how long it will be retained. Additionally, it requires explicit, informed, and freely given consent from individuals prior to the processing of their personal data, thereby tightening the control individuals have over their personal data.

Furthermore, the principle of data protection by design and default, introduced in the GDPR, has embedded accountability deeper into organisational structures. This principle requires data protection safeguards to be integrated into products and services from the outset, ensuring data protection becomes an intrinsic part of the organisational culture. It promotes the minimization of data collection, limiting access to personal data, and ensuring the anonymity of data subjects.

The governance of data protection in the UK is implemented by the Information Commissioner's Office (ICO). The ICO is an independent authority set up to uphold information rights in the public interest, promote openness by public bodies, and oversee data privacy for individuals. It has the power to administer penalties for non-compliance, including significant fines. Good governance in data protection, therefore, requires organisations to maintain an ongoing dialogue with the ICO, comply with its guidelines, and report any data breaches promptly.

Organisations are also encouraged to obtain certification schemes or codes of conduct approved by the ICO. These provide practical guidance on how to comply with the law and can act as a mitigating factor if an organisation is investigated for a data breach. These measures further enhance the governance of data protection in the UK, promoting a proactive approach to data protection compliance.

In conclusion, accountability and governance are not only the cornerstones of data protection in the UK, but also an ongoing responsibility for organisations. They require organisations to put robust mechanisms in place, conduct regular audits, continuously train staff on data protection matters, and stay updated on changes in the regulatory landscape. This ensures that data protection is not seen as a one-time event, but a continual process that is integrated into everyday organisational activities and culture.

Therefore, while the DPA 2018 and the GDPR have undoubtedly set high standards for accountability and governance in data protection, they are, in essence, promoting a culture of respect for personal data. This is pivotal in an increasingly digitised world, where data breaches can have severe consequences for individuals and organisations alike. Thus, ensuring robust accountability and governance in data protection is not just a legal obligation, but also a moral and ethical necessity.

Data protection in the workplace

Data protection in the workplace is a fundamental aspect of operating a business in the United Kingdom. With the rapid advancement of digital technology, the amount of data generated and processed by organisations has grown exponentially. This increased reliance on data, particularly sensitive personal information, necessitates the implementation of robust data protection measures to ensure the integrity, confidentiality and availability of data.

In the UK, data protection in the workplace is primarily governed by the General Data Protection Regulation (GDPR) and the Data Protection Act 2018. The GDPR establishes a regulatory framework that aims to standardise and enhance data protection within the European Economic Area (EEA), while the Data Protection Act 2018 supplements and tailors the GDPR within the UK context. Together, these pieces of legislation provide an over-arching and comprehensive approach to data protection and privacy.

At the heart of these regulations is the principle of 'lawfulness, fairness and transparency'. This principle mandates that data should be processed in a lawful, fair and transparent manner in relation to the data subject. This means that organisations should be clear about why they are collecting data, what they intend to do with it, and how long they plan to keep it. Furthermore, they should only collect data for specified, explicit and legitimate purposes and not process it further in a way that is incompatible with those purposes.

Another important principle is 'data minimisation', which stipulates that personal data collected should be adequate, relevant and limited to what is necessary in relation to the purposes for which they are processed. This underscores the necessity of not collecting more information than is required. Employers should therefore review the data they collect to ensure it is not excessive and that it is kept up to date.

The principle of 'integrity and confidentiality', commonly known as the security principle, is also a cornerstone of data protection. This principle requires that appropriate technical and organisational measures are taken to protect personal data against unauthorised or unlawful processing, accidental loss, destruction or damage.

In the workplace, these principles translate into a variety of practical measures. To begin with, organisations should conduct a data protection impact assessment (DPIA) when initiating new projects or implementing new technologies. A DPIA is a process that helps organisations identify and minimise the data protection risks of a project.

Further to this, the role of a Data Protection Officer (DPO) is instrumental in ensuring compliance with data protection regulations. The DPO is responsible for overseeing data protection strategy and implementation, educating employees about compliance, conducting regular security audits, and serving as the point of contact between the company and any Supervisory Authorities.

Moreover, employers should establish clear policies and procedures for data protection and ensure their employees are adequately trained on these. This includes guidelines on secure data storage, use of passwords, encryption, secure disposal of data, and responding to data breaches.

In terms of individual rights, employees have the right to access their personal data held by their employer, to request the rectification if the data is inaccurate and to object to processing in certain circumstances. These rights further underscore the importance of transparency and accuracy in data handling.

While the penalties for non-compliance are significant, including heavy fines and reputational damage, a strong commitment to data protection in the workplace goes beyond mere compliance. It helps cultivate trust, demonstrating to employees, customers and stakeholders that their personal information is respected and protected.

To sum up, data protection in the UK workplace is a complex area, requiring a comprehensive understanding of the legal requirements and practical measures necessary to ensure compliance. It is a dynamic, evolving challenge, one that requires continuous monitoring and adjustment to ensure that the safeguards put in place are robust and effective.

Children's data protection

The Data Protection Act 2018 (DPA 2018) is the UK's legislation for the protection of personal data, with regulations regarding how organisations handle data, how it is processed, stored and shared. Crucially, this law also includes provisions specifically tailored to the protection of children's personal data, recognising the vulnerability of children and the need to afford them higher levels of protection in relation to their personal data.

Under DPA 2018, the term 'children' refers to individuals under the age of 18. This act asserts that children have the same rights as adults over their personal data and how it is used. These rights include the right to be informed about how their data is used, the right to access their data, the right to rectify if their data is inaccurate, the right to erase data, the right to restrict processing, the right to data portability, the right to object and rights in relation to automated decision-making and profiling.

The DPA 2018 sets a high standard for what constitutes 'consent' when processing children's personal data. It stipulates that consent must be given or authorised by the holder of parental responsibility if the child is under the age of 13. This means that the organisation must make reasonable efforts to verify that the person giving consent does hold parental responsibility. The Act also states that any privacy notice should be written in a language that children can understand, ensuring they are aware of how their data will be used.

The Act also introduces special categories of children's data, which includes genetic data, biometric data and data concerning health, sex life or sexual orientation. For processing this category of data, explicit consent is required. It means the consent should be freely given, specific, informed and unambiguous, reflecting the higher level of protection provided by the Act.

When it comes to direct marketing, decision making or profiling, the Act outlines that the organisation must not only consider how to protect children from potential harm but also whether the child understands what is involved. If a child is not competent to understand, they are deemed unable to give consent.

In regards to data breaches, the Act includes provisions that oblige data controllers to report data breaches involving children's personal data to the UK's Information Commissioner's Office (ICO) within 72 hours of becoming aware of it. This report must include details of the breach, the possible consequences, and what mitigating actions have been taken.

Under DPA 2018, the ICO has the power to issue fines of up to £17 million or 4% of global turnover, whichever is higher, for organisations that fail to comply with the regulations concerning children's data protection. Additionally, the ICO can also implement other corrective measures such as warnings, reprimands or orders to bring processing operations into compliance.

The DPA 2018 also encourages the use of Data Protection Impact Assessments (DPIAs) when processing children's personal data. DPIAs are designed to help organisations identify and minimise the data protection risks of a project. They are particularly relevant when a new data processing technology is being introduced, or when a profiling operation is likely to significantly affect individuals.

Children's data protection under the DPA 2018 also involves cross-border data transfers. If children's personal data is being transferred outside the UK, additional safeguards must be in place. This can include adequacy decisions, where the ICO has determined that the country or organisation provides an adequate level of data protection, or appropriate safeguards such as legally binding and enforceable agreements between public authorities or bodies.

In summary, the Data Protection Act 2018 provides a comprehensive framework for the protection of children's data in the UK, legislating consent requirements, special category data, direct marketing and data breaches. This framework not only serves to protect children but also holds organisations accountable for their handling of children's personal data.

CCTV and data protection in the UK

In the United Kingdom, Closed Circuit Television (CCTV) is extensively utilised in various domains, from public areas like parks and streets to private properties such as homes and offices. This prevalent use of surveillance technology has necessitated the implementation of stringent data protection laws to safeguard the rights, privacy and data of individuals. The correlation between CCTV and data protection in the UK presents a unique intersection of security and privacy rights, mandating an intricate balance between surveillance necessity for public safety and preserving the individual's right to privacy.

The use of CCTV in the UK is primarily regulated by the Data Protection Act 2018 (DPA) and the General Data Protection Regulation (GDPR). These legislations play a pivotal role in outlining the framework that dictates how personal data obtained through CCTV can be collected, stored, processed, and shared. Therein, 'personal data' refers to any information that could be used to identify an individual, which, in the context of CCTV, would include any footage where individuals can be recognised.

Under the DPA and GDPR, any individual or organisation that uses CCTV to collect personal data assumes the role of a "data controller". As data controllers, they are legally bound to comply with the principles of data protection. These principles primarily revolve around the lawful, fair and transparent collection and processing of data. They emphasise that the collection of data should be for a legitimate purpose and the least amount of data necessary for that purpose should be collected. The data should not be kept for longer than necessary and should be securely stored with adequate protections against unauthorised access, accidental loss, damage or destruction.

A key element of data protection legislation in the UK is the provision of rights to individuals about whom data is collected. These rights include the right to be informed about the collection and use of their data, the right to access this data, the right to rectification if the data is inaccurate, the right to erasure (also known as 'the right to be forgotten'), the right to restrict processing, the right to data portability, the right to object to data processing, and rights related to automated decision making and profiling. In the context of CCTV, this typically means that individuals have the right to know that CCTV is in operation (usually through clear signage), to request access to footage of themselves, and to request the deletion or correction of any footage that is inaccurate.

As per the Information Commissioner's Office (ICO) in the UK, which is the independent authority set up to uphold information rights in the public interest, the usage of CCTV must be justified and proportionate. This means the benefits that will be gained, such as deterrence of crime, must be more substantial than any perceived intrusion of an individual's privacy. If CCTV is used, the ICO recommends conducting a Data Protection Impact Assessment (DPIA) to help data controllers identify and minimise any data protection risks associated with the use of CCTV.

Compliance with data protection legislation is crucial, as failure to comply can lead to significant penalties. Non-compliance with the DPA can result in fines of up to £17 million or 4% of the organisation's global turnover, whichever is higher.

However, it's not just the risk of fines that organisations need to consider. There can also be substantial reputational damage resulting from non-compliance, resulting in loss of trust and confidence from the public or customers. Therefore, it is not just a legal obligation, but also a moral and business imperative to ensure that the use of CCTV complies with data protection law.

In summary, the use of CCTV in the UK is intricately intertwined with data protection legislation. The DPA and GDPR provide a robust framework for the lawful, fair and responsible collection, storage and processing of personal data obtained through CCTV. They underscore the need to respect and uphold individuals' rights, while striking a delicate balance between the need for security and the preservation of privacy.

Direct marketing and data protection in the UK

Direct marketing is a form of advertising where businesses communicate directly to customers through a variety of media, including phone calls, text messages, emails, websites, online adverts, database marketing, fliers, catalogue distribution, promotional letters, and targeted television, newspaper and magazine advertisements. In the United Kingdom, this brand of marketing plays a significant role in promoting goods and services to the end consumer, allowing businesses to target specific audiences, measure responses and results accurately, and fine-tune marketing strategies based on these insights.

However, the practice of direct marketing has been considerably influenced by the evolution of data protection laws in the UK. The Data Protection Act 2018 (DPA 2018) and the European Union's General Data Protection Regulation (GDPR), which took effect in May 2018, have laid down stringent rules and regulations on how companies can collect, store, process and use personal data.

The DPA 2018 requires businesses to follow several key principles of data protection. These include ensuring that personal data is used fairly, lawfully and transparently, used for specified, explicit purposes, used in a way that is adequate, relevant and limited to only what is necessary, accurate and kept up to date, kept for no longer than is necessary, and handled in a way that ensures appropriate security, including protection against unlawful or unauthorised processing, access, loss, destruction or damage.

In the context of direct marketing, this means that businesses must obtain consent from individuals before they can use their personal data for marketing purposes. Consent must be freely given, specific, informed, and there must be an indication signifying agreement. It cannot be inferred from silence, pre-ticked boxes or inactivity. Importantly, individuals have the right to withdraw consent at any time.

Moreover, under the GDPR, individuals have the right to object to the processing of their personal data for direct marketing purposes at any time, free of charge. If an individual makes such an objection, the business must immediately stop processing their data for these purposes.

The Information Commissioner's Office (ICO) in the UK is responsible for upholding information rights and enforcing these data protection laws. It has the power to issue significant fines to businesses that breach the regulations – up to £17 million or 4% of a company's total worldwide annual turnover, whichever is higher.

The Privacy and Electronic Communications Regulations (PECR) also contain specific rules on marketing calls, emails, texts and faxes, cookies (and similar technologies), and the security of public electronic communications services in the UK. PECR is derived from European law and sits alongside the Data Protection Act and the GDPR.

Under PECR, businesses must have an individual's consent to send them marketing emails, texts or conduct live marketing phone calls. For automated marketing calls, the individual must have specifically agreed to receive them unless the number is withheld.

In light of these regulations, it is clear that direct marketing strategies in the UK must be carefully crafted to ensure compliance with data protection laws. Businesses need to take into account the rights and freedoms of individuals when planning their marketing activities, diligently observing their obligations in terms of data collection, storage, processing and use.

Moreover, businesses must maintain clear records of how and when an individual gave consent, and what they were told at the time. This is necessary to demonstrate compliance with both the DPA 2018 and GDPR, should the business's data processing activities be called into question.

In conclusion, the interplay between direct marketing and data protection in the UK is complex, requiring a thorough understanding of the legal landscape and an ability to navigate the intricacies of regulatory compliance. Failure to do so can result in severe financial penalties, reputational damage, and a loss of consumer trust, all of which can have a detrimental impact on a business's bottom line and future growth prospects.

Data protection in healthcare

In the United Kingdom, data protection within the healthcare sector is a matter of considerable importance. It's a facet of the industry that requires consistent and meticulous attention, not only due to the sensitive nature of the information, but more so due to the critical role it plays in facilitating efficient patient treatment and care.

Data protection in the healthcare sector primarily serves to safeguard the confidentiality, integrity, and accessibility of patient data. This entails ensuring that personal health information is only accessed by authorised individuals, that the information is accurate and free from corruption, and that it is readily available when required.

The Data Protection Act 2018, a pivotal piece of legislation in the UK, governs data protection across all sectors including healthcare. This act essentially aligns the UK's data protection framework with the General Data Protection Regulation (GDPR) of the European Union, while also outlining exemptions and modifications specific to the UK context. As such, it's a comprehensive law covering all aspects of data protection – from principles and rights of individuals to enforcement procedures.

At the core of data protection in the healthcare sector are seven key principles. These include lawfulness, fairness, and transparency; purpose limitation; data minimisation; accuracy; storage limitation; integrity and confidentiality (security); and accountability. Every entity involved in the processing of health data, whether NHS trusts, private clinics, or healthcare app providers, are bound by these principles.

To ensure the lawful and fair processing of health data, healthcare providers must have a legitimate reason for collecting and using personal data. Furthermore, they are obliged to be open and clear about how they intend to use this data. The purpose limitation principle, meanwhile, stipulates that health data should only be collected for explicit, legitimate purposes and not used beyond these defined purposes.

The principle of data minimisation calls for the collection and processing of only what is necessary. In essence, healthcare entities must ensure that the personal data they collect is adequate, relevant, and limited to what is necessary in relation to the purposes for which they are processed. Alongside this, the accuracy principle dictates that healthcare providers must take all reasonable steps to rectify or delete inaccurate health data.

Storage limitation, on the other hand, implies that personal health data should not be held for longer than necessary. As per this principle, healthcare providers must also have a system in place for timely data deletion. Where the integrity and confidentiality principle is concerned, it necessitates that health data must be kept secure. This involves protecting it from unauthorised or unlawful processing, accidental loss, destruction, or damage.

Lastly, the accountability principle places an obligation on healthcare providers to be responsible for, and able to demonstrate compliance with, the other data protection principles. This entails implementing appropriate technical and organisational measures, carrying out data protection impact assessments, and assigning a data protection officer where needed.

The rights of individuals in the context of data protection in healthcare are equally significant. These include the right to be informed, the right of access, the right to rectification, the right to erasure, the right to restrict processing, the right to data portability, the right to object, and rights in relation to automated decision-making and profiling.

Failure to comply with the Data Protection Act 2018 can result in severe penalties. The Information Commissioner's Office (ICO), the UK's independent authority set up to uphold information rights, has the power to issue fines of up to £17 million or 4% of global turnover, whichever is higher, for serious breaches.

The complexities of data protection in the healthcare sector further amplify due to the advent of digital technologies. The growing use of electronic health records, wearable devices, and telemedicine, for instance, poses new challenges in maintaining data privacy and security. This necessitates a continuous review and adaptation of data protection policies and practices to align with technological advancements and evolving threats.

In conclusion, data protection in healthcare is a multifaceted aspect, woven with legislative, technological, and ethical implications. It requires a proactive and vigilant approach to ensure that the personal health data of individuals is protected whilst also facilitating efficient and effective healthcare delivery.

Data protection in education

Data protection in education in the UK is a critical subject that has gained prominence in recent years due to the increased digitisation of the education sector. It revolves around the processes, regulations, and methods employed to guard the information of students, staff, and stakeholders from unauthorised access, manipulation, corruption, loss, or disclosure. The concept also entails the policies for data use and storage implemented by the educational institutions or the relevant authorities.

One of the significant laws governing data protection in education is the Data Protection Act (DPA) of 2018, which aligns with the General Data Protection Regulation (GDPR). This act lays out clear guidelines for how personal information should be handled within an educational setting. It includes stringent stipulations on data consent, data breaches, and hefty penalties for non-compliance. It also introduces concepts such as the 'right to be forgotten', which empowers individuals to have their personal data erased.

GDPR emphasises the importance of obtaining explicit consent from the individuals (or their parents or guardians, in the case of minors) before collecting and processing their personal data. This implies that educational institutions must thoroughly explain why and how they would use the data, offering an option to withdraw consent at any time. This is particularly crucial in the context of student data, as it often includes sensitive information about the student's academic records, behaviour, health, and well-being.

Data breaches are a significant concern for educational institutions, considering the vast amounts of sensitive data they handle. GDPR mandates that any data breach that poses a risk to individuals' rights and freedoms must be reported to the Information Commissioner's Office (ICO) within 72 hours of becoming aware of it. Failure to do so may result in severe penalties, including fines of up to 4% of the institution's annual global turnover or €20 million, whichever is higher.

In addition to the regulations, educational institutions have an ethical responsibility to ensure data protection. Schools, colleges, and universities are trusted with sensitive information by students, parents, and staff, who expect their personal information to be handled with care and integrity. The misuse or mishandling of this data can lead to significant consequences beyond the legal implications, including loss of reputation and trust.

The UK's Department for Education (DfE) has provided a toolkit for schools to help them understand and comply with the requirements of the GDPR and the DPA 2018. This includes guidelines on data mapping, identifying data protection officers, executing privacy impact assessments, and understanding individuals' rights concerning their data.

Emerging technologies such as cloud computing and big data analytics pose new challenges to data protection in education. While these technologies offer numerous benefits, including cost savings, enhanced efficiency, and improved learning outcomes, they can also introduce new vulnerabilities. Educational institutions must therefore employ robust cybersecurity measures and regularly update their data protection policies and strategies to effectively manage these risks.

Data protection training for staff is another essential aspect of data protection in education. Staff members, from administrators to teachers, often handle sensitive data.

Equipping them with the knowledge and skills to handle this data securely and appropriately can significantly reduce the risk of data breaches or other mishandlings. Regular training sessions, webinars, and workshops can serve as effective platforms to educate staff about their roles and responsibilities concerning data protection.

Indeed, data protection in education in the UK is a multifaceted issue that demands a comprehensive and proactive approach. It requires a careful balance between harnessing the benefits of digital technology in education and ensuring the security and privacy of personal data. While statutory regulations such as the DPA and GDPR provide a robust framework for data protection, it ultimately falls upon the educational institutions themselves to ensure strict adherence and foster a culture of data protection within their premises.

Data protection in financial services

Data protection in the financial services sector in the UK is an issue of paramount importance, one that demands a robust and comprehensive approach. It is a terrain that requires both a firm grasp of technological nuances and a judicious interpretation of legal and regulatory directives. The financial services sector, due to its very nature, has at its disposal a wealth of sensitive personal and financial data. This makes it a prime target for unscrupulous cybercriminals, necessitating stringent data protection measures.

The regulatory framework for data protection in the UK is primarily constituted by the Data Protection Act 2018 (DPA 2018) and the General Data Protection Regulation (GDPR). These legal instruments outline the principles, rights, and obligations for most processing of personal data. The DPA 2018 was designed to supplement the GDPR, tailoring the latter's general regulations to the specific context of the UK, and additionally covering areas of data protection that fall outside the GDPR's scope.

The most salient provisions of the GDPR and DPA 2018 applicable to the financial sector relate to the lawful processing of data, rights of the data subjects, data breach notification, accountability and governance, and transfer of data.

Financial services firms must ensure the lawful processing of data. They must have a legal justification for processing personal data, whether it is based on consent, contract, legal obligation, protection of vital interests, public interest, or legitimate interests. The concept of 'legitimate interests' is particularly significant in the financial sector. It could be invoked, for instance, when a bank shares customer data with a credit reference agency to assess creditworthiness or with law enforcement agencies to prevent fraud.

The rights of data subjects include right of access, right to rectification, right to erasure, right to restrict processing, right to data portability, right to object, and rights related to automated decision making and profiling. Financial firms must uphold these rights unless there is a compelling reason not to, such as the need to comply with other legal obligations or to establish, exercise or defend legal claims.

In the event of a data breach, financial services institutions are required to notify the Information Commissioner's Office (ICO) without undue delay, and where feasible, within 72 hours of becoming aware of the breach. If there is a high risk to the rights and freedoms of the data subject, they must also notify the affected individuals without undue delay.

Firms are expected to demonstrate compliance with the data protection principles. This includes maintaining relevant documentation on processing activities, implementing data protection by design and by default, conducting data protection impact assessments for high-risk processing, and appointing a data protection officer if required.

Cross-border data transfers are subject to additional rules. If a financial services firm in the UK wishes to transfer personal data to a country outside the European Economic Area (EEA), it must ensure adequate safeguards. These include Standard Contractual Clauses, Binding Corporate Rules, or reliance on an adequacy decision by the European Commission.

In the financial services sector, the Financial Conduct Authority (FCA) also has a role in overseeing data protection compliance. While the ICO is the lead authority for data protection, the FCA expects firms to observe the GDPR and DPA 2018 as part of their obligation to treat customers fairly and use their information responsibly.

The FCA and ICO have also collaborated on a joint guide for firms, outlining how the two regimes work together. It emphasizes the importance of sharing information with statutory and regulatory bodies for the prevention and detection of financial crime, while ensuring that such sharing is fair, transparent, and in compliance with the law.

The landscape of data protection in the UK's financial services sector is dynamic and multifaceted, shaped by the interplay of technological advancements, evolving cyber threats, and shifts in regulatory norms. Financial institutions striving to navigate this landscape must adopt a proactive and holistic approach, integrating legal compliance with technological resilience and ethical data stewardship.

Data protection in social media

Data protection in social media in the UK is an intricate subject matter that requires an exhaustive understanding of the prevailing laws, regulations, and relevant industry practices. It is a realm that necessitates vigilance, transparency, and respect for user rights in the collection, processing, and sharing of personal data.

In recent years, the United Kingdom has taken a proactive approach to data protection, primarily under the General Data Protection Regulation (GDPR), which was enacted in May 2018. The UK's embodiment of GDPR is the Data Protection Act 2018, which embodies the same principles, rights, and obligations, and maintains its relevance even as the UK has exited the European Union.

At the heart of the Data Protection Act is the concept of 'personal data', which refers to any information that can be used to identify a living individual directly or indirectly. This broad definition encompasses a vast array of data, especially in the context of social media where user-generated content, profile information, and network interactions generate a wealth of identifiable data.

Social media platforms operating in the UK are held to high standards in the way they manage their users' personal data. They are expected to gain explicit, informed consent from users before collecting their data, providing clear indications of what data is being collected and for what purposes. Essentially, users must understand the data agreement they are entering into and must be given the chance to opt out without consequence.

In addition, data minimisation is a central tenet in the UK's approach to data protection. This principle requires social media companies to only collect data that is necessary for the specified purpose, thereby preventing excessive data collection. Furthermore, the data must be kept accurate and up-to-date, and must be erased or rectified when no longer necessary for the purpose.

The Data Protection Act also enshrines data subject rights. This ensures that individuals have the right to access their data, rectify inaccuracies, and have their data erased in certain circumstances, often referred to as 'the right to be forgotten'. This extends to social media, and individuals can request access to all the personal data a social media platform holds on them.

Moreover, social media platforms are obliged to ensure the security of the personal data they hold. This requires adequate security measures to prevent data breaches, which could have severe consequences for users' privacy. The UK's Information Commissioner's Office (ICO) oversees and enforces data protection compliance, with the power to levy hefty fines for violations.

However, the enforcement of data protection in social media is fraught with challenges. Social media platforms are global entities, often based beyond UK jurisdiction, which adds layers of complexity to enforcement. Furthermore, the dynamic and evolving nature of social media platforms, with their ever-changing algorithms and data practices, keep them moving targets for regulation.

Despite these challenges, the UK remains committed to upholding data protection on social media. The recent Online Safety Bill signals the government's intent to impose a duty of care on social media companies to protect their users from harmful content, which extends to violations of privacy and data protection. This heralds a new era of regulatory scrutiny over social media, underpinned by the enduring principles of the Data Protection Act.

In conclusion, data protection in social media in the UK is a multifaceted issue, interweaving legal, technological, and societal aspects. It's a dynamic landscape shaped by evolving legislation, emerging technology trends, and shifting user expectations – a landscape that demands unswerving commitment to transparency, respect for user rights, and an unflagging pursuit of privacy protection.

Data protection in research

Data protection in research within the United Kingdom is a pivotal cornerstone that governs the collection, storage, handling, and dissemination of personal data. It revolves around a complex matrix of principles, laws, and guidelines that aim to protect the rights and privacy of individuals, ensuring that their personal information is not misused or exploited.

Primarily, the Data Protection Act 2018 (DPA 2018) governs data protection in the UK. It provides a comprehensive framework that defines the manner in which personal data should be handled. The Act details eight principles, including fairness and lawfulness, purpose limitation, data minimisation, accuracy, storage limitation, integrity and confidentiality, accountability, and the rights of the data subject.

The first principle, fairness and lawfulness, mandates that any data collected must be done so fairly and lawfully. Researchers must be transparent about the data being collected, how it is to be used, who will have access to it, and the measures in place to ensure its security. Purpose limitation ensures that data collected in research is used explicitly for the purpose stated and not for any other unrelated purposes. It implies that data must not be processed in a manner incompatible with those purposes.

The principle of data minimisation asserts that only pertinent, adequate, and necessary data, relevant to the research, should be collected and processed. It holds that there should be no superfluous collection or storage of data. The accuracy principle necessitates that personal data should be exact, current, and updated. Storage limitation stipulates that personal data should not be retained longer than needed.

Integrity and confidentiality require data handlers to safeguard personal data, ensuring protection against unlawful processing, accidental loss, destruction, or damage. The accountability principle underscores that data controllers are responsible for, and must be able to demonstrate, compliance with the other principles. The rights of the data subject affirm that individuals have the right to be informed, the right of access, the right to rectification, the right to erasure, the right to restrict processing, the right to data portability, the right to object, and the rights in relation to automated decision making and profiling.

Moreover, the UK's General Data Protection Regulation (UK GDPR) is another crucial framework, which came into effect from January 1, 2021, post-Brexit. It largely mirrors the European Union's GDPR, and together with the DPA 2018, sets out the main responsibilities for organisations in relation to data protection.

The UK GDPR mandates that data processors and controllers implement adequate technical and organisational measures to ensure data protection principles are integrated into processing activities. This concept of 'data protection by design and by default' encourages researchers to consider data protection issues at the outset of any project involving personal data.

Furthermore, the UK GDPR also introduced a requirement to report certain types of data breach to the Information Commissioner's Office (ICO), and in some cases to the individuals affected. The ICO is the UK's independent authority, set up to uphold information rights in the public interest, promoting openness by public bodies and data privacy for individuals.

Another critical aspect in the UK is the Research Ethics Committees (RECs), which play a vital role in scrutinising research proposals involving personal data. These committees evaluate the ethical implications of research projects, ensuring that the privacy and rights of individuals are adequately protected.

Explicit consent is another cornerstone of data protection in research within the UK. Individuals must provide unambiguous, informed, and explicit consent for their data to be collected and used in research. This consent must be freely given and can be withdrawn at any time.

In summary, data protection in research in the UK is a multi-faceted and comprehensive domain, underpinned by a robust legal framework. It involves an intricate network of principles, laws, regulations, and guidelines, all designed to ensure the safeguarding of personal data, the upholding of individual's rights, and the promotion of ethical research practices. It is incumbent upon all researchers to adhere to these standards, thereby fostering trust, integrity, and privacy in the pursuit of knowledge and understanding.

Data protection in law enforcement

In the UK, the scope of data protection within the realm of law enforcement is both comprehensive and multifaceted. Governed by a suite of robust legislative frameworks, it plays an integral role in the intricate balance between the preservation of individual privacy and the safeguarding of public security.

At the forefront of these legislative pillars is the Data Protection Act 2018 (DPA 2018), which reflects the EU's General Data Protection Regulation (GDPR) and the Law Enforcement Directive, with a specific part of the Act (Part 3) dedicated to law enforcement processing. This third part of the DPA 2018 regulates the processing of personal data by competent authorities for law enforcement purposes, encompassing activities such as the prevention, investigation, detection, or prosecution of criminal offences or the execution of criminal penalties.

In essence, the DPA 2018 sets out strict principles for data processing, mandating that data must be processed lawfully, fairly, and transparently, collected for explicit and legitimate purposes, be adequate, relevant, and not excessive, accurate and up to date, kept only as long as necessary, and processed securely. In terms of law enforcement, these principles are particularly pertinent, given the sensitive nature of the data often handled, including genetic or biometric data.

The Information Commissioner's Office (ICO) is the UK's independent authority responsible for enforcing these standards, ensuring that law enforcement agencies adhere to the data protection principles when processing personal data. In the event of non-compliance, the ICO possesses the power to impose penalties, such as fines and other sanctions.

Further, the UK law enforcement agencies are obliged to conduct a Data Protection Impact Assessment (DPIA) for processing operations that are likely to result in high risk to the rights and freedoms of individuals, including systematic monitoring, processing of sensitive data on a large scale, or public monitoring on a large scale. This assessment becomes a significant tool in identifying and minimising the data protection risks of a project.

Moreover, the DPA 2018 also imposes restrictions on international transfers of data for the purposes of law enforcement. Any such transfer must be necessary for the prevention, detection, or prosecution of criminal offences and must meet specific adequacy and safeguarding requirements.

Despite Brexit, the UK has expressed the intention to maintain alignment with EU data protection laws, acknowledging that international cooperation in the fight against crime and terrorism often requires the sharing of personal data. The recently concluded EU-UK Trade and Cooperation Agreement includes provisions to enable such data sharing for law enforcement while respecting data protection and privacy rights.

In addition, the role of the UK's intelligence services in data protection cannot be overlooked. The Investigatory Powers Act 2016 provides a legal framework for their powers to obtain communications data from telecoms operators, subject to rigorous safeguards and oversight mechanisms, including the role of the Investigatory Powers Commissioner's Office.

In conclusion, the UK's data protection landscape in law enforcement is characterised by a complex web of legislation that strives to protect individual privacy rights while ensuring that law enforcement agencies can function effectively. Despite this, the legal framework is continually evolving to respond to new challenges and technological advances, demonstrating the UK's commitment to maintaining a robust and dynamic approach to data protection in the realm of law enforcement.

Data protection impact on AI and machine learning

The importance of data protection in relation to artificial intelligence (AI) and machine learning cannot be overstated, particularly in the context of the United Kingdom. The ever-increasing reliance on these technologies in both businesses and public services has necessitated a thorough examination of the implications for privacy rights and data protection.

One of the primary concerns is the sheer volume of personal data processed by AI and machine learning systems. Given that these technologies rely on large datasets to train their algorithms and improve their accuracy, they inherently involve the collection, storage and utilisation of significant amounts of data. This is particularly concerning when this data is sensitive in nature, such as health records, financial details or other personal identifiers.

The UK's Data Protection Act 2018, which complements the General Data Protection Regulation (GDPR) implemented by the European Union, has introduced several measures to regulate the use of such technologies. These include the requirement for data minimisation and purpose limitation, which mandate that only the minimal necessary data should be processed, and only for specific, explicit and legitimate purposes. These measures are intended to prevent the indiscriminate collection and use of personal data.

Moreover, the Act introduces the concept of 'data protection by design and default', which necessitates that data protection measures are integrated into the design of AI and machine learning systems. This means that privacy considerations should be front and centre in the development process, rather than being an afterthought. This approach encourages a proactive stance on data protection, rather than a reactive one.

Another key aspect of the legislation is the right to explanation. This means that individuals have the right to understand how decisions that affect them are made by automated systems. This is particularly relevant for machine learning algorithms, which are often described as 'black boxes' due to their complex and opaque nature. However, this right to explanation is still a subject of debate, given the technical challenges in explaining the decision-making processes of complex AI systems.

The UK's Information Commissioner's Office (ICO), the regulatory body for data protection, has also issued guidelines on AI and data protection. The ICO emphasises the need for transparency, data minimisation, security and accountability when processing personal data for AI purposes. In particular, the ICO stresses the importance of conducting Data Protection Impact Assessments (DPIAs) when using AI. These assessments are meant to identify and minimise the data protection risks of projects, particularly when processing sensitive data or utilising new technologies.

However, despite these regulations and guidelines, there are still challenges to be tackled. One significant issue is the international nature of AI and machine learning. Data is often transferred across borders for processing and storage, which creates complexities in terms of jurisdiction and enforcement. Given the global nature of many technology companies, the UK must work in concert with international partners to ensure consistent data protection standards.

Furthermore, the rapid development of AI and machine learning technologies can often outpace regulatory efforts. As these technologies advance and become more pervasive in society, the potential for misuse of personal data also increases. This necessitates ongoing vigilance and adaptation of regulations to keep pace with technological innovations.

The impact of data protection on AI and machine learning in the UK is therefore multifaceted. It is a balancing act between harnessing the benefits of these technologies, and ensuring the protection of individual privacy rights. While the existing regulations provide a robust framework for data protection, the dynamic nature of AI and machine learning necessitates continuous reassessment and updating of these policies to ensure they remain fit for purpose.

Data protection and cloud computing

Cloud computing, a transformative technology, is becoming increasingly popular in the business world and is reshaping the manner in which organisations conduct their operations. However, it also presents a myriad of data protection issues that require astute consideration, especially within the regulatory landscape of the United Kingdom.

At the heart of these issues is the need to ensure the privacy and security of data. Individuals and organisations are often sceptical about the migration of sensitive information from a local storage system to a remote cloud server. This apprehension is not without reason; the remote nature of cloud computing can potentially expose data to various risks such as unauthorised access, loss of data, or even cyber attacks.

The Data Protection Act 2018 (DPA) and the General Data Protection Regulation (GDPR) are the primary pieces of legislation governing data protection in the United Kingdom. The DPA applies the EU's GDPR standards making UK law compatible with a fast digital economy. Within this regulatory framework, organisations are required to implement appropriate technical and organisational measures to ensure the security of personal data.

For cloud service providers operating in the UK, compliance with these regulations is obligatory. To this end, they are required to provide a high level of security for their services, ensuring that data is not only stored securely but also transmitted securely over the internet. This involves the use of encryption techniques to protect data in transit and at rest, as well as robust access control measures to prevent unauthorised access.

Moreover, data protection law in the UK mandates the adoption of a privacy by design and by default approach. This necessitates the integration of data protection measures into the design of cloud computing systems and services, rather than as an addition. For instance, the choice of cloud computing model, be it a public, private or hybrid cloud, has implications for how data is managed and protected. Therefore, careful consideration should be given to the selection and implementation of the most suitable model for the specific needs of an organisation.

In addition, there are stringent requirements regarding the transfer of personal data outside the European Economic Area (EEA) which directly impacts cloud services. Consequently, when UK-based organisations use a cloud service that involves transferring personal data outside the EEA, they must ensure appropriate safeguards are in place. These safeguards typically take the form of binding corporate rules or standard contractual clauses that bind the parties to protect the privacy and security of the data.

Data breach notification is another crucial aspect of data protection in the context of cloud computing. The GDPR mandates that in the event of a data breach, organisations are required to notify the relevant supervisory authority within 72 hours of becoming aware of the breach. This requirement emphasises the need for effective incident response procedures to detect, report and investigate a personal data breach.

Additionally, the use of cloud computing services necessitates a clear and comprehensive contract between the cloud service provider and the user. This contract, often referred to as a cloud services agreement, should clearly stipulate the responsibilities and liabilities of each party with respect to data protection. This includes the handling, storage and transfer of data, and the measures in place to protect the data from loss, damage or unauthorised access.

UK law also ascribes significant importance to the concept of data minimisation. This principle stipulates that personal data should be adequate, relevant and limited to what is necessary in relation to the purposes for which it is processed. This signifies that organisations should only collect, process and store the minimal amount of personal data necessary for their operations.

Thus, while cloud computing offers numerous benefits in terms of cost savings, scalability and flexibility, it also presents significant challenges related to data protection. In the UK, these challenges are addressed through a comprehensive legal and regulatory framework that aims to balance the benefits of cloud computing with the need for robust data protection. Compliance with this framework is not only a legal obligation for organisations that use cloud services, but also a means of building trust with customers and stakeholders, and maintaining a favourable business reputation.

Data protection and biometrics

In the progressive era of technology where data proliferation is rapidly escalating, the United Kingdom is not left behind in traversing the trajectory. With the advent of biometric technology, a significant shift is observed in the landscape of data protection in the UK.

Primarily, biometrics refers to the technology that measures and analyses human physical and behavioural characteristics for authentication, identification, or access control. These characteristics could include fingerprints, iris scans, voice recognition, and facial patterns. As biometric data is unique to each individual, it carries substantial weight in terms of personal identification, making it a significant focal point for protection under data protection laws.

The principal legislation governing data protection in the UK is the Data Protection Act 2018 (DPA 2018), supplemented by the General Data Protection Regulation (GDPR). The DPA 2018 provision makes it clear that biometric data used for identifying an individual is classified as 'special category data', implying that it requires a higher level of protection than other personal data.

In light of this, the law mandates organisations to meet specific conditions before processing this type of data. This includes obtaining explicit consent from the data subject, ensuring that processing is necessary for carrying out obligations under employment, social security or social protection law, or safeguarding the individual's vital interests where the data subject is physically or legally incapable of giving consent.

Data protection and biometrics in the UK also involve the robust involvement of the Information Commissioner's Office (ICO), the

UK's independent authority set up to uphold information rights. The ICO provides guidance and regulations that help organisations, including those relying on biometrics, navigate the complex terrain of data protection. It ensures that the principles of GDPR such as lawfulness, fairness, transparency, data minimisation and accuracy, among others, are upheld when processing biometric data.

The application of biometrics, while proving to be a powerful tool in enhancing security measures, has raised substantial privacy concerns. For instance, in public surveillance, the use of facial recognition technology has been a topic of heated debate, with critics arguing that it infringes on the privacy rights of individuals. The courts and the ICO are continually working to strike a balance between the benefits of biometrics and the potential invasion of privacy.

In the context of employment, the use of biometric data presents another domain where the principles of data protection are to be robustly applied. Employers adopting biometric systems, such as fingerprint scanning for timekeeping, must ensure they comply with the data protection laws. This includes informing employees about the collection and use of their biometric data, explaining the purpose behind it, and obtaining their explicit consent.

The UK is also making strides in applying biometrics in the banking and finance sector. Enhanced security measures are necessary to protect sensitive financial information, and biometrics plays a significant role here. Measures like fingerprint recognition, voice ID, and facial recognition are increasingly being used. As these technologies continue to evolve, care must be taken to ensure data is processed securely, once again highlighting the role of legislation like the DPA 2018 and the GDPR.

In conclusion, data protection and biometrics in the UK represent an intricate tapestry of technological advancement and legislative oversight. The application of biometric technology is set to grow, and with it, the importance of robust data protection measures. While the legislation provides a robust framework, the challenge lies in its application, ensuring that the use of biometrics does not compromise the privacy rights of individuals.

Data protection and cybersecurity

In the United Kingdom, data protection and cybersecurity are fundamental considerations for all individuals and entities handling digital information. These areas are governed by stringent regulations that ensure the integrity, confidentiality, and availability of data.

The UK Data Protection Act 2018, the main legislation that governs the handling and protection of personal data in the country, creates binding obligations for anyone involved in data processing. The Act establishes a solid framework for the protection of personal data, laying out principles that must be adhered to in the processing of such data. These principles encompass the lawful, fair and transparent processing of data; limitation of data processing to specific, explicit and legitimate purposes; minimisation of data to that which is necessary; accuracy of data; restrictions on storage periods; and the conducting of data processing in a manner that ensures its security.

Parallel to the Data Protection Act is the General Data Protection Regulation (GDPR), a Europe-wide legislation that has been incorporated into UK law. GDPR extends the scope of data protection to all entities that handle the data of EU citizens, irrespective of their domiciliary location.

In terms of cybersecurity, the UK's approach is multifaceted, with efforts concentrated on promoting cybersecurity awareness, enhancing the country's cyber capabilities, and fostering cooperation between public and private sectors. The National Cyber Security Centre (NCSC), a subsidiary of the Government Communications Headquarters (GCHQ), is at the forefront of the UK's cybersecurity strategy. The NCSC provides guidance and support to the public and private sectors in managing cyber threats, while also working to improve the country's cyber resilience.

To bolster its cybersecurity framework, the UK government has also implemented the Network and Information Systems (NIS) Regulations 2018. These regulations aim to improve the security of network and information systems across the country, with a particular focus on critical infrastructure sectors such as energy, transport, healthcare, and digital services.

Alongside these regulations, the UK government has developed the Cyber Essentials scheme, a certification pathway for businesses to demonstrate their adherence to cybersecurity best practices. The scheme outlines basic controls that organisations should implement to mitigate cyber threats, such as secure configuration, boundary firewalls, access controls, malware protection, and patch management.

The UK's legal framework for data protection and cybersecurity is supplemented by a robust enforcement regime. The Information Commissioner's Office (ICO), as the UK's independent authority set up to uphold information rights, has the power to impose significant fines on entities that violate data protection laws.

Furthermore, the Serious Crime Act 2015 provides for severe penalties, including imprisonment, for those involved in cybercrimes. This Act has broadened the scope of computer misuse offences, elevating the unauthorised acts that impair the operation of computers, hinder access to programs or data, or enable the commission of further offences.

In tandem with these legislative measures, the UK has actively pursued international cooperation in the areas of data protection and cybersecurity. It is a signatory to the Budapest Convention on Cybercrime, which fosters international cooperation in the investigation and prosecution of cybercrime.

In conclusion, the UK boasts a robust framework for data protection and cybersecurity, underpinned by comprehensive legislation, vigilant enforcement, and an active commitment to international cooperation. These elements coalesce to form a formidable bulwark against data breaches and cyber threats, ensuring the safety and integrity of personal data within the digital realm.

Data protection and the GDPR

The landscape of data protection in the United Kingdom is one that has seen substantial changes in recent years, the most significant of which was the introduction of the General Data Protection Regulation (GDPR) in 2018. As an initiative of the European Union, the GDPR has been designed with the fundamental intention of providing individuals with greater control over their personal information, contextually transforming the way organisations handle and manage data.

In the wake of the UK's departure from the European Union, the importance of GDPR has not diminished, but rather evolved. The Data Protection Act 2018, which incorporates the provisions of the GDPR, remains in force in the UK, ensuring that the principles of GDPR continue to underpin data protection laws in the country.

The crux of data protection under the GDPR and the UK's own legislation revolves around several key principles. The first of these is lawfulness, fairness, and transparency. This principle obliges organisations to process personal data lawfully and clearly, without misleading individuals about the purpose for which their data is being used.

The principle of purpose limitation stipulates that personal data can only be collected for specified, explicit, and legitimate purposes. This means that organisations must be clear from the outset about why they are collecting data and what they intend to do with it. Data minimisation is another key principle, which dictates that organisations should only collect and process the data that is necessary for the purposes they have stated.

Accuracy is a critical factor in data protection. The GDPR requires that personal data must be accurate and, where necessary, kept up to date. This means that organisations must take reasonable steps to ensure that inaccurate data is rectified or deleted without delay.

Another key principle is storage limitation, which mandates that personal data should not be kept in a form which permits identification of data subjects for longer than is necessary for the purposes for which the data is processed. To adhere to this principle, organisations need to establish time limits for erasure or for a periodic review of the data they hold.

The GDPR also enshrines the principle of integrity and confidentiality, better known as the duty to secure personal data. Organisations are required to implement appropriate technical and organisational measures to protect against unauthorised or unlawful processing, accidental loss, destruction, or damage of data.

The concept of 'accountability' is another cornerstone of the GDPR. It requires that organisations take responsibility for the data they hold and how they handle it, demonstrating compliance with all the other principles of data protection.

One of the most lauded aspects of the GDPR is the power it grants to individuals over their personal data. Under the regulation, individuals have a number of rights, including the right to be informed about how their data is used, the right to access their data, the right to correct inaccurate data, the right to have personal data erased, and the right to restrict or object to the processing of their data.

It's worth noting that while the GDPR sets out these principles, it also gives national authorities some flexibility to tailor certain aspects of the rules to their own context. In the UK, the Information Commissioner's Office (ICO) is the independent authority set up to uphold information rights, promoting openness by public bodies and data privacy for individuals. The ICO has a key role in enforcing and regulating the compliance with GDPR in the UK.

In conclusion, data protection in the UK, underpinned by the principles of the GDPR and overseen by the ICO, is a robust framework designed to safeguard personal data. It places stringent obligations on organisations, while empowering individuals with rights over their personal information. The landscape may continue to change, particularly in light of the UK's exit from the EU, but the importance of secure, fair, and transparent data processing will remain paramount.

Data protection and human rights

In the United Kingdom, the intersection of data protection and human rights is a topic of considerable importance, marked by a dense weave of legal frameworks, statutory regulations, and practical considerations. From the standpoint of legislative provisions, the most significant instrument addressing this area is the Data Protection Act 2018, which provides a comprehensive set of rules designed to protect individuals' personal data.

This Act represents the UK's implementation of the European Union's General Data Protection Regulation (GDPR), which was designed to modernise laws that protect the personal information of individuals. The Act itself outlines the key principles, rights, and obligations for most processing of personal data. Its primary aim is to secure individuals' data rights, including the right to be informed about how their data is used, the right to access that information, the right to object to direct marketing, and rights in relation to automated decision making and profiling.

Notwithstanding its importance, the Data Protection Act is not the only relevant piece of legislation. The Human Rights Act 1998, which incorporates the European Convention of Human Rights into UK law, enshrines the right to respect for private and family life, home, and correspondence in Article 8, which is a fundamental principle in any discussion of data protection.

This respect for private life is interpreted broadly and includes the right to establish and develop relationships with other human beings and the outside world and can sometimes involve a duty on the government to protect this right. Importantly, it also encompasses the control individuals have over their personal data and the way in which that data is accessed and disseminated.

In the practical realm, data protection is not solely a matter of legal compliance; it is also an issue of ethical responsibility. There is an increasing expectation from the public that organisations not only conform to the letter of the law in terms of data protection but also that they demonstrate genuine respect for personal privacy and individual autonomy. This involves choices about what data is collected in the first place, how it is stored, who has access to it, and how it is used.

In the financial sector, for instance, data protection is integral to maintaining trust between institutions and their customers. Banks and financial institutions handle vast amounts of sensitive personal data, and the breach of data privacy can have severe consequences, both in terms of legal penalties and the erosion of customer trust.

In the healthcare sector, too, data protection is pivotal. Patient data must be handled with the utmost care, respecting confidentiality and protecting against any unauthorised access or usage. The healthcare professionals are under both a legal duty and a professional obligation to ensure patient data is treated with the respect it deserves.

Privacy in the context of law enforcement and national security presents another crucial facet to the data protection discussion. While the authorities must have the necessary powers to prevent crime and protect national security, these powers must be balanced with individuals' rights to privacy. This delicate balance is often at the heart of controversies surrounding surveillance practices and intelligence gathering.

Data protection and human rights in the UK are also greatly influenced by technological advancements. With the rise of digital platforms, social media, and AI, the scope of data collection broadens, and the potential for misuse or abuse of personal data increases. This rapidly changing landscape continually and consistently challenges existing laws and regulations and calls for their constant evaluation, revision, and adaptation.

In conclusion, the nexus of data protection and human rights in the UK is deeply complex, involving a myriad of laws, regulations, sectors, and ethical dilemmas. As technology evolves and the amount of data generated expands, the task of protecting personal data while respecting human rights will continue to be both critically important and extraordinarily challenging.

Data protection and freedom of expression

In the UK, the sphere of data protection and freedom of expression is a complex and multifaceted construct, borne out of the interplay between various pieces of legislation, case law, and human rights principles. The most significant legal instruments in this area are the Data Protection Act 2018 (DPA), the General Data Protection Regulation (GDPR), and the Human Rights Act 1998 (HRA), which implements the European Convention on Human Rights (ECHR) into UK law.

The DPA 2018 and GDPR provide the foundation for the way personal data is protected in the UK. These pieces of legislation contain principles, rights, and obligations pertaining to the handling of personal data, which is defined as any information relating to an identifiable individual. Under these laws, entities that process personal data – be they individuals, companies, or public bodies – must comply with a set of rigorous obligations. These include, amongst others, the requirements to process personal data lawfully, fairly, and in a transparent manner; to collect personal data for specified, explicit, and legitimate purposes; and to ensure that any personal data processed is adequate, relevant, and limited to what is necessary for the purposes for which it is processed.

At the same time, the DPA 2018 and GDPR contain provisions aimed at safeguarding the right to freedom of expression. Article 85 of the GDPR, for instance, requires Member States to reconcile the right to the protection of personal data with the right to freedom of expression and information. Similarly, the DPA 2018 recognises that processing of personal data for journalistic purposes, or for the purposes of academic, artistic, or literary expression, should be subject to a more relaxed regime, provided such processing is necessary for the purposes of exercising the right to freedom of expression.

Meanwhile, the HRA 1998 incorporates into UK law the fundamental rights and freedoms contained in the ECHR, including the right to respect for private and family life (Article 8) and the right to freedom of expression (Article 10). These rights are not absolute, and need to be balanced against each other and other competing rights. In the context of data protection and freedom of expression, this often involves a delicate balancing act between protecting individuals' privacy and allowing for open and robust public debate.

The balance is often struck on a case-by-case basis, taking into account the specific facts and circumstances of each situation. Courts in the UK, for instance, have repeatedly emphasised the need to balance the right to privacy under Article 8 ECHR with the right to freedom of expression under Article 10 ECHR, particularly in cases involving the media and the press. In doing so, they have often had to grapple with thorny questions such as the public interest in the information being disseminated, the potential harm caused by the disclosure of personal data, and the means by which the data was obtained.

Case law has shown that the balance can tilt in favour of either right, depending on the circumstances. In some instances, courts have prioritised the right to privacy, citing the need to protect individuals from intrusive or unwarranted interference with their personal lives. In other cases, the right to freedom of expression has prevailed, with courts recognising the important role played by the media in a democratic society, and the necessity of allowing for the free flow of ideas and information.

In addition to these legal instruments, the Data Protection Authority, known as the Information Commissioner's Office (ICO), plays a crucial role in enforcing data protection laws and ensuring respect for the right to freedom of expression in the UK. The ICO has the power to impose hefty fines on entities that breach data protection laws, and issues guidance on how to comply with the requirements of the DPA 2018 and GDPR. At the same time, the ICO recognises the importance of the right to freedom of expression, and has published guidance on how these rights interact in practice.

In conclusion, data protection and freedom of expression in the UK are governed by a complex framework of laws, case law, and regulatory guidance. This framework seeks to strike a balance between protecting individuals' personal data and preserving the right to freedom of expression. The balance is not always easy to achieve, and is often subject to scrutiny and debate. Nonetheless, the existence of such a framework is testament to the UK's commitment to upholding these fundamental rights and freedoms.

Data protection and the right to access information

Situated at the heart of contemporary society, the concept of data protection and the right to access data has become an indispensable pillar of the legal structure in the United Kingdom. This simultaneous right to privacy and access to information is primarily governed by the Data Protection Act 2018 (the Act), which is nuanced with a complex web of clauses and conditions that seek to strike a delicate equilibrium between transparency and confidentiality.

The Act is a complex but essential piece of legislation. It basically sets out rules for processing personal information and applies to certain activities, such as computerised processing, paper filing systems and even access to publically available information. The Act encompasses a scope that is broad and far-reaching, extending its influence from large corporations handling thousands of data elements daily to individuals processing personal data in their homes.

The Act confers a number of rights on individuals, central to which is the right to access personal data. This right allows individuals to be aware of and verify the lawfulness of the processing of their personal data. Through a Subject Access Request (SAR), individuals can request a plethora of information, including the purposes for processing their personal data, the categories of personal data concerned, and the recipients to whom the personal data have been or will be disclosed.

On the other hand, the Act also empowers organisations with certain responsibilities concerning the processing of personal data. These responsibilities, termed the seven key principles, require organisations to process personal data lawfully, fairly and transparently, collect it for specified and legitimate purposes, ensure it is adequate, relevant and limited, and update it where necessary. They also mandate that organisations store personal data for no longer than necessary, protect it appropriately, and bear the onus of demonstrating compliance with these principles.

As with any prominent legislation, the Act is not devoid of challenges and obstacles. One of the most significant is the dilemma of navigating the fine line between the data subject's right to privacy and the public's right to access information. This is a delicate balance to achieve, often leading to legal debates and conflicts. For example, whilst the Freedom of Information Act 2000 provides public access to information held by public authorities, it must be weighed against the data protection principles, especially when the information sought relates to identifiable individuals.

To facilitate this balancing act, the Information Commissioner's Office (ICO), the UK's independent authority set up to uphold information rights, provides guidance to organisations on how to comply with the law. It has the power to issue hefty fines to those who fall foul of the Act, thus providing a significant deterrent to non-compliance.

Moreover, the Act is underpinned by the principle of 'data minimisation', which stipulates that personal data must be adequate, relevant and limited to what is necessary in relation to the purposes for which they are processed. This principle, however, can sometimes clash with the increasing demand for Big Data, where large volumes of information are analysed computationally to reveal patterns, trends, and associations.

In an increasingly digital age, the UK has also had to adapt its data protection laws in line with international standards, particularly the General Data Protection Regulation (GDPR). The

Act endeavours to ensure a smooth transition in the post-Brexit era, incorporating the GDPR into UK law to ensure continuity of data protection standards.

Overall, the intriguing interplay between data protection and the right to access information in the UK is a dynamic and ever-evolving field. It is characterised by a constant struggle to balance individual privacy rights with the need for transparency and access to information, necessitating careful navigation through the labyrinthine landscape of data protection law. The constant advances in data technology only serve to make this task more challenging, yet exciting, for lawmakers, data processors, and data subjects alike.

Data protection and e-commerce

In the realm of digital trade, or e-commerce, the UK stands as a vibrant hub, incessantly pulsating with a myriad of online transactions every second. However, within this bustling digital marketplace, the issue of data protection holds a paramount role, defining the trust between consumers and businesses while forming the legal framework which shapes the operations of e-commerce.

Data protection in e-commerce encompasses several aspects, the first of which is the collection and use of personal data. For every online transaction, personal data such as names, addresses and financial information are essential components. This data is inevitably stored and processed by the e-commerce platforms, making it susceptible to misuse or breach. Hence, the UK's Data Protection Act 2018, which aligns with the EU's General Data Protection Regulation (GDPR), stipulates strict guidelines for data collection, processing, and storage.

The Act mandates that companies must clearly inform customers about the type of data being collected and the purpose behind it. They must also ensure that sufficient consent is obtained before processing the data. Notably, the Act also entitles individuals to access the data companies hold about them and challenge inaccurate or misleading information. These legal obligations, while forming a strong foundation for the online business framework, also pose stringent challenges for e-commerce businesses in the UK. They have to constantly innovate and implement robust data protection measures to stay compliant with these legislations.

Furthermore, the cross-border flow of data, a quintessential feature of e-commerce, also falls under the remit of data protection laws. The UK's exit from the EU, or Brexit, has cast its effect on this aspect. Despite the UK aligning its data protection laws with the GDPR, the transfer of data between the UK and EU member states is no longer as seamless. The UK has been granted an adequacy decision by the EU, which means the EU recognises the UK's data protection standards as equivalent to its own. Yet, the decision is subject to review and can be revoked, adding a layer of uncertainty to future data transfers.

Cybersecurity is another crucial facet in the data protection-e-commerce matrix. The escalation of cyber threats and the increasing sophistication of cybercriminals pose significant threats to e-commerce businesses and online consumers. The UK government has taken active measures to combat these threats. The establishment of the National Cyber Security Centre and the enforcement of the Network and Information Systems Regulations 2018 are indicative of the UK's commitment to bolstering its cyber defences.

These measures require companies to have robust systems in place to prevent and respond to cyber-attacks, thereby ensuring the safety of customer data. The regulations also mandate companies to report significant cyber incidents to competent authorities, promoting transparency and accountability. But, for e-commerce businesses, these added obligations can mean increased costs and complexity of operations. They must allocate resources for installing advanced cybersecurity systems, training personnel, and staying updated with the evolving cyber threat landscape.

The implications of data protection for e-commerce businesses in the UK extend beyond compliance to influence customer trust and reputation. In a world where data breaches and misuse of personal information are rife, a strong data protection regime can substantially determine an e-commerce business's success. A robust data protection policy can enhance consumer confidence, fostering loyalty and repeat business. On the other hand, any lapse in data protection can lead to severe reputational damage and significant financial penalties.

In conclusion, the realm of data protection and e-commerce in the UK is a complex yet crucial landscape. It is marked by stringent laws, evolving cyber threats, the implications of Brexit, and the central role of customer trust. Navigating this landscape requires e-commerce businesses to remain vigilant, innovative, and committed to upholding the highest standards of data protection.

Data protection and the Internet of Things (IoT)

As the Internet of Things (IoT) continues to proliferate across the United Kingdom, the issue of data protection stands out as one of the paramount concerns. IoT refers to the network of interconnected devices that communicate and exchange data with each other over the internet. These devices, which range from everyday household appliances like refrigerators and thermostats to industrial machinery and wearable technology, generate vast amounts of data. This incessant flow of data, if not adequately protected and managed, could potentially be exploited, leading to privacy breaches and various other security complications.

The Data Protection Act 2018 (DPA 2018), which replaced DPA 1998, forms the cornerstone of the UK's data protection legislation. Incorporating the EU General Data Protection Regulation (GDPR), it sets out the framework for data protection law in the UK, mandating that data must be processed lawfully, transparently, and for a specific purpose. Data processed must also be accurate and up to date, held securely, and retained for no longer than necessary.

The DPA 2018 also establishes eight data protection principles, which IoT stakeholders must adhere to. These include ensuring data is obtained fairly and lawfully, that data is held for specified and lawful purposes, and that data is not transferred to countries outside the European Economic Area without adequate protection.

The Information Commissioner's Office (ICO), an independent UK authority, plays a crucial role in regulating and enforcing these data protection laws. The ICO's role extends to educating the public about their rights, investigating complaints and taking enforcement action when necessary. It has the power to impose hefty fines on organisations that fail to comply with data protection regulations.

In the realm of IoT, data protection takes on a new level of complexity. IoT devices are often designed for convenience and improved functionality and thus may overlook critical aspects of data protection. Many devices collect a considerable amount of personal data, often without the user's explicit knowledge or consent. This data can be highly sensitive, including details about a person's habits, preferences, movements and even health status.

Moreover, the interconnected nature of IoT devices presents additional security risks. A vulnerability in one device could potentially compromise the entire network, leading to widespread data breaches. As such, securing the IoT ecosystem requires a robust and comprehensive approach.

The UK Government has recognised these challenges and in January 2020, it introduced a proposal for mandatory security requirements for consumer IoT devices. These include unique device passwords, a public point of contact for vulnerability reporting, and explicitly stating the minimum length of time for which the device will receive security updates.

Additionally, organisations must invest in data encryption technologies, use secure data transfer protocols, and regularly update their devices and systems to guard against potential vulnerabilities. They must also focus on 'privacy by design', which involves building data protection principles into the design of IoT devices and systems right from the start of the development process, rather than treating it as an afterthought.

Despite these measures, the rapid pace of technological advancement and the burgeoning IoT landscape continue to pose significant challenges to data protection in the UK. Therefore, vigilance, education, and a culture of data protection and data privacy are vital in navigating the complexities of this rapidly-evolving digital landscape.

Data protection and big data analytics

In the contemporary digital age, the role of data protection and big data analytics in the UK cannot be overestimated. Both have become cornerstones of numerous industries, from finance and healthcare to marketing and research, underpinning critical business decisions and strategies.

Data protection in the UK is regulated primarily by the General Data Protection Regulation (GDPR), an EU regulation that took effect in May 2018, and the UK's Data Protection Act 2018, which complements the GDPR and provides specific provisions for the UK context. These regulations have greatly bolstered the protection of personal data, emphasising the principles of accountability, transparency, and the importance of obtaining explicit consent before collecting and using personal data.

The GDPR in particular has been revolutionary, changing the landscape of data protection in the UK and beyond. It enshrines the rights of individuals about their personal data, including the right to access, correct, erase, restrict, move, and object to the processing of their data. These rights have given individuals unprecedented control over their personal data, empowering them to dictate how and when their data is used.

For organisations, these regulations have imposed strict obligations and penalties, inducing them to improve their data protection practices. Organisations are now required to implement robust data protection measures, demonstrate their compliance with the regulations, and promptly report any personal data breaches.

Big data analytics, on the other hand, refers to the process of examining vast and varied data sets, or 'big data', to unearth hidden patterns, correlations, and insights. It is a powerful tool that has the potential to transform businesses, drive innovation, and improve decision-making. In the UK, big data analytics is widely used across a range of sectors, from banking and retail to healthcare and public services.

In the banking sector, for instance, big data analytics is harnessed to detect fraudulent transactions, assess credit risk, and personalise customer services. In the retail sector, it is used to understand customer behaviour, optimise logistics, and tailor marketing campaigns. In healthcare, big data analytics can help in predicting disease outbreaks, improving patient care, and advancing medical research.

Despite its tremendous potential, the use of big data analytics presents several challenges. One of these is the issue of data privacy. With big data analytics involving the processing of massive amounts of data, some of which may be personal, there is a risk that data privacy could be compromised. This is where data protection comes in, providing a framework for managing the risks associated with big data analytics.

Another challenge is the risk of bias in data analytics. If the data used in the analysis is biased, the results will also be biased, leading to flawed decisions and potentially discriminatory practices. To mitigate this risk, organisations need to ensure that their data is representative and that their analytical models are transparent and fair.

In addition, the use of big data analytics requires significant technical expertise and resources. Analysing big data is a complex task that requires advanced analytical tools and techniques, such as machine learning and artificial intelligence. For many organisations, particularly small and medium-sized enterprises (SMEs), it can be difficult to acquire these capabilities.

Despite these challenges, the benefits of big data analytics are immense, and the UK is well-positioned to reap these benefits. The UK has a strong data infrastructure, a vibrant tech sector, and a robust regulatory framework for data protection. With the right strategies and safeguards in place, the UK can harness the power of big data analytics while protecting the privacy and rights of individuals.

Data protection and government surveillance

The realm of data protection in the UK is a labyrinthine landscape ruled by intricate legal and ethical frameworks, as well as a host of government and independent bodies. As the digital age has matured, so too has the realisation that our personal data – those nuggets of information that define our identities, preferences, habits and secrets – has become an increasingly valuable commodity. This has led to a dual-edged sword in which the government, on one hand, has had to implement measures to protect individuals' data, while on the other hand, it has come under scrutiny for its surveillance activities.

The main legislation guiding data protection in the UK is the General Data Protection Regulation (GDPR), which came into effect in May 2018. Quite a mouthful, the GDPR is an EU regulation that the UK has adopted into its law, providing a robust framework for the protection of personal data. The crux of this regulation lies in its insistence that organisations who handle personal data must do so responsibly, transparently and with explicit consent from the individual in question.

This has given rise to a myriad of changes in how UK organisations collect, store, and handle data, forcing them to be more transparent with individuals about the type of data they collect and how it is used. Infringements of these rules can result in hefty fines, thus instilling a sense of accountability and vigilance amongst organisations. The Information Commissioner's Office (ICO), as an independent authority, has been set up to uphold these information rights, enforcing the GDPR and dealing with complaints from individuals.

This evolving landscape of data protection is further complicated by issues of government surveillance. The UK government, like many others around the world, has been repeatedly criticised for its controversial mass surveillance programmes. A key player in the 'Five Eyes' intelligence alliance, the UK's Government Communications Headquarters (GCHQ) has been implicated in various global surveillance programmes, such as the PRISM and Tempora operations, which were revealed by the whistleblower Edward Snowden.

The Investigatory Powers Act of 2016, often dubbed the 'Snooper's Charter', has only heightened these concerns. This law allows the government to legally monitor the internet usage of its citizens, intercept communications, and collect bulk data. The Act not only empowers a wide range of government bodies to access this data but also requires Internet Service Providers (ISPs) to store the browsing histories of all their users for a year. This legislation has been met with intense criticism from privacy advocates and human rights organisations, who argue that such sweeping powers infringe on civil liberties and the right to privacy.

While proponents of government surveillance argue that such measures are necessary to ensure national security and fight terrorism, critics contend it is an invasion of privacy and can easily lead to abuse of power. There have been significant legal challenges to the Investigatory Powers Act, notably from civil liberties group Liberty, which argues the Act breaches human rights. The challenge led to the Appeal Court ruling in January 2019 that parts of the Act were indeed unlawful.

Moreover, the intersection of government surveillance and data protection legislation presents a complex paradox. On the one hand, the GDPR emphasises the right to personal privacy and the protection of personal data. On the other hand, the Investigatory

Powers Act seems to fly in the face of these principles by enabling mass data collection and surveillance.

In this complex landscape, it is clear that the balance between data protection and government surveillance in the UK is a delicate one, fraught with continual ethical, legal and technological challenges. As the digital age continues to evolve, so too will these issues, demanding ever-greater scrutiny, debate and legislation to ensure the right balance between personal privacy, data protection and national security.

Data protection and employment in the UK

Data protection in the UK is a topic of paramount importance that has not only legal implications, but also ethical and societal ones. It is guarded by a myriad of laws, regulations, policies, and best practice guidelines that are aimed to protect the rights of individuals and ensure organisations comply with their obligations in relation to data processing activities. One area where data protection is particularly relevant is within the context of employment.

Employment in the UK involves the processing of a significant volume of personal data. This encompasses everything from basic information such as names and contact details, to sensitive data like health records, criminal convictions, trade union membership, or data concerning race or ethnicity. The handling of such personal and sensitive data requires appropriate care, diligence and compliance with relevant legislation to safeguard the employees' privacy rights.

Foremost in the UK's data protection landscape is the General Data Protection Regulation (GDPR), which came into effect across the European Union (EU) in May 2018. Despite the UK's departure from the EU, these regulations continue to apply, with the government incorporating the GDPR into UK law under the Data Protection Act 2018. This act, alongside the Employment Practices Data Protection Code, provides the main framework for data protection in the workplace.

One of the key principles of the GDPR is data minimisation, which stipulates that personal data collected should be adequate, relevant and limited to what is necessary in relation to the purposes for which they are processed. In the employment context, this implies that employers should only collect and process data that is necessary for them to fulfil their contractual obligations, comply with legal requirements, or serve a legitimate interest.

Moreover, consent is a central component of the GDPR, requiring organisations to obtain explicit, informed consent from individuals before collecting, using or sharing their personal data. In the employment setting, obtaining meaningful consent can be challenging due to the inherent power imbalance between employers and employees.

The GDPR also introduces stringent accountability and transparency requirements. Employers are required to maintain detailed records of their data processing activities, implement appropriate technical and organisational measures to ensure data security, and provide clear information to employees about how their data will be used, who it will be shared with, and how long it will be kept.

Transparency is paramount; employees must be informed of the data being gathered, the purpose of its collection, the period for which it will be retained, and their rights with respect to their personal data. They have the right to access their data, correct inaccuracies, have their data erased, restrict the processing of their data, and object to the processing of their data in certain circumstances.

In addition, the ICO (Information Commissioner's Office) plays a pivotal role in data protection in the UK. This independent authority upholds information rights, promotes openness by public bodies, and data privacy for individuals. The ICO has the authority to enforce the provisions of the GDPR and the Data Protection Act 2018, including the power to issue significant fines for non-compliance.

In the realm of employment, the complexity of data protection is further compounded by other considerations, such as monitoring in the workplace and the use of social media. Monitoring can range from CCTV surveillance and monitoring of email or internet use, to more sophisticated methods such as the use of AI or biometric data. Given the intrusive nature of these practices, employers must carefully balance their legitimate interests, such as theft prevention or maintaining productivity, against the privacy rights of their employees.

In conclusion, data protection and employment in the UK is a multifaceted field, rooted in a complex maze of legislation, case law, and best practice guidelines. It's a sphere that demands constant vigilance, robust policies, and a culture of respect for the privacy rights of employees.

Data protection and social responsibility

In the interconnected world of today, data has become the lifeblood of virtually every industry and sector. It's the fuel that powers our digital economy, guides the decision-making process of businesses, and enables governments to provide better services to their citizens. However, as data becomes more integral to society, the issue of data protection and social responsibility inevitably comes to the forefront. This is particularly relevant in the UK, a nation which prides itself on upholding values of fairness, integrity and respect for the rights and freedoms of individuals.

Data protection in the UK is governed by the Data Protection Act 2018, which has replaced the Data Protection Act 1998, and is supplemented by the General Data Protection Regulation (GDPR). This comprehensive regulatory framework sets out strict rules about collecting, storing, processing, and sharing personal data. It establishes fundamental rights for individuals over their personal data, including the right to be informed about how their data is used, the right to access their data, the right to rectify inaccuracies, and the right to erasure, commonly known as 'the right to be forgotten'. Breaches of these laws can result in severe penalties, including hefty fines.

In the age of Big Data, where vast amounts of information can be collected and analysed with just a few clicks, the role of businesses in maintaining data protection is more crucial than ever. Companies are expected to be transparent about their data practices, ensuring that they obtain proper consent from individuals before collecting their data, and that they use this data responsibly and for the purposes it was collected. This requires comprehensive data protection policies and robust systems to safeguard personal data from breaches and misuse.

The social responsibility aspect of data protection in the UK encompasses a broad spectrum of considerations and obligations. It encompasses the duty of companies to respect the privacy of individuals, to handle their personal data with the utmost care, and to implement measures to prevent unauthorized access, data breaches, and other threats to data security. Additionally, it involves the ethical use of data, ensuring that it is not used to perpetuate discrimination, exploitation, or harm to individuals or groups in society.

To exemplify, a company that utilises targeted advertising should do so in a manner that respects the privacy and personal preferences of individuals. They should not exploit sensitive personal data, such as health information, in ways that could disadvantage or discriminate against individuals. Similarly, organisations that use algorithms or artificial intelligence to make decisions that affect individuals, such as credit scoring or job recruitment, have a responsibility to ensure that their systems are fair, transparent, and do not result in unjust bias or discrimination.

Moreover, the social responsibility aspect extends to the role of companies in contributing to the development of a digital society that is inclusive, fair, and respects human rights. This includes initiatives to bridge the digital divide, promote online safety and digital literacy, and support the use of data and digital technologies for social good, such as in health, education, and environmental sustainability.

This is compounded by the need for businesses to consider the global implications of their data activities. In an interconnected world, the collection and use of data by UK companies can have far-reaching effects on individuals and societies beyond the UK's borders. This necessitates a global perspective and an understanding of international data protection standards and practices.

Furthermore, it is important to consider the role of the UK government in data protection and social responsibility. The government has a key role in establishing and enforcing data protection laws, and in shaping the digital landscape through policies and regulations. It also has a responsibility to lead by example in its own use of data, whether in public services, policymaking, or other areas of government activity.

In conclusion, data protection and social responsibility in the UK involve a complex interplay of legal, ethical, and societal considerations. It's a multifaceted issue that calls for ongoing vigilance, commitment, and innovation from all stakeholders in society. As the digital landscape continues to evolve, so too must the approaches and strategies for protecting data and upholding social responsibility.

Printed in Great Britain
by Amazon

46542456R00069